The Evaluation of Aid Projects and Programmes

Proceedings of the Conference organised by the
Overseas Development Administration in the
Institute of Development Studies,
at the University of Sussex
7–8 April 1983

Editor: Dr. B. E. Cracknell
Head, Evaluation Department

OVERSEAS DEVELOPMENT ADMINISTRATION
ELAND HOUSE, STAG PLACE, LONDON SW1E 5DH

338.9162
OVE
①
10/84

ISBN 0 11 580243 6

Printed in the UK for HMSO   Dd716940 C50 4/84 (796)

Contents

Foreword by the Rt Hon Timothy Raison MP, Minister of State for Foreign and Commonwealth Affairs and Minister for Overseas Development

At over £1100 million per annum, Britain's official aid programme is a substantial one. It is spent through a number of channels and our direct bilateral finance goes to more than 120 different developing countries. The administration of our aid is a complex task and we are continually looking for means to improve its effectiveness. This is all the more important when tax-payers' money and public accountability are concerned.

As part of the efforts of the Overseas Development Administration (ODA) to this end, the work of our Evaluation Department has a high standing among the professionals in this field. I am pleased that their work, through this record of the proceedings of the Conference, will now be made available to a wider audience. The Conference—the first of its kind held in Britain—provided a forum for the ODA to describe its evaluation programme and some of the approaches being developed. Our objective in evaluation is to enable lessons to be learned from the experience of implementing development projects and programmes; then to be sure these lessons are applied to new decisions and passed on to governments and their advisers in the developing world who can translate this information into ultimate benefits for their populations. Evaluation work tests in all respects the concepts and systems used, and in doing so the mistakes and successes of professionals and others engaged in the development process are critically examined. Only in this way can developing countries and donors be satisfied that the assistance is achieving the objectives intended.

The Conference was very successful, and I hope that these proceedings will encourage a productive exchange of ideas and experience between those active in development, including our fellow aid donors.

TIMOTHY RAISON

Introduction

This book is based on the papers (and the discussions arising from them) presented at the ODA Conference on Evaluation held in the Institute of Development Studies at the University of Sussex, 7–8 April 1983. The Conference was attended by 140 specially invited participants, including evaluators, consultants, academics, representatives of developing countries and evaluation experts from bilateral and multilateral institutions. In all there were 30 participants from overseas. The Conference took the form of a series of brief presentations of previously distributed papers followed by opportunities for discussion after each presentation.

In the interest of producing a readable text a fair degree of editorial licence has been exercised, particularly with regard to the contributions to the discussion, so that the gist has not been lost but hopefully the presentation is crisper and in a more orderly sequence.

Readers may be interested to know that at the Conference the ODA arranged a display of one-page evaluation summaries called 'EVSUMs' and that copies of two ODA publications were made available to all participants. These were *ODA's Evaluation Activities 1982* (a list of all completed ODA evaluation reports) and *The Lessons of Experience*, a booklet summarising some of the key lessons learned from ODA's evaluation studies. Copies of all these publications may be obtained, free of charge, from the Evaluation Department, Overseas Development Administration, Eland House, Stag Place, London SW1E 5DH.

The editor, Dr B. E. Cracknell, Head of the Evaluation Department, ODA, would be pleased to receive any comments on the contents of this book. One of its main purposes is to encourage a wider dialogue between people interested in evaluation issues, not only among the main donor agencies but especially between them and the developing countries which are increasingly becoming aware of the importance of evaluation, whether it be sponsored by donor agencies or not.

PART

ODA'S EVALUATION PROCEDURES AND PROBLEMS

A1

The Organisation of Evaluation Work in ODA by Dr B. E. Cracknell, Head, Evaluation Department, ODA

The evaluation work in ODA has recently been reorganised and given an enhanced status, and as the staffing and organisation of an evaluation department raises a number of problems it is worth dwelling briefly on the experience to date.

Evaluation work in ODA began on a small scale and the initiative came from the Economic Planning Service who wanted to find out how effective the newly developed project appraisal procedures were proving in practice. Thus most of the early evaluation work of ODA was carried out by the economists, and the full-time staff of the Evaluation Unit were all economists until 1981 when the first administrator was added to the complement. However, long before this it was realised that evaluation calls for a wide range of expertise and this is obtained partly by commissioning studies by outside consultants and partly by using ODA's own staff (especially advisers) on temporary release from their normal duties.

By 1982 the volume of evaluation work had increased so substantially that some reorganisation became necessary. Up to that time the volume of work had not justified a full-time Senior Economic Adviser, so an adequate workload was achieved by combining two units, the Evaluation Unit and the Manpower Planning Unit (MPU), into the one 'Manpower and Evaluation Department', of which I was Head. By 1982 the evaluation work had grown to the point where this linking of two units with different functions had become unnecessary, and it was therefore decided to separate the MPU and to upgrade the Evaluation Unit to the Evaluation Department.

The second major change was the decision to transfer the day-to-day management of the evaluation programme to an administrative principal. The economists had been getting too involved in administrative work. Under this new structure they are able to concentrate on giving economic advice on evaluations to the administrator and are available to participate as members of evaluation teams. It was thus decided that the Evaluation Department would be an integrated administrative/professional group headed by a Senior Economic Adviser reporting to the Under Secretary supervising the Aid Policy and Finance Division. The economists retain their professional links within the Economic Service. This is a fairly unusual structure in Civil Service terms, although there are a number of other examples. It seems to fit the particular requirements of evaluation work very well.

The Evaluation Department annually submits its work programme to the ODA's Projects and Evaluation Committee (PEC) for their comments and approval. This Committee, which scrutinises and advises the Minister on all significant new spending decisions in the bilateral programme, also receives and discusses all individual evaluation reports. The organogram of the Evaluation Department looks like this:

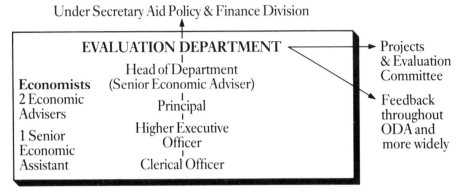

The three main tasks of the Evaluation Department are (1) to plan and implement a programme of about 20 evaluations per annum, with a budget to cover commissioned studies (plus travel expenses of in-house staff) of £325 000 per annum; (2) to organise a programme of feedback of the results of evaluations; (3) to liaise with evaluation departments of other aid agencies.

1 Planning and Implementing the Evaluation Programme

There is a consistent pattern to most evaluation studies except perhaps those that relate to ODA's internal procedures. The first step in setting up an evaluation programme is to 'trawl' the office asking for suggestions for projects to evaluate (against the sort of criteria laid down by the PEC and described in Chapter A4), and then to present the list (with detailed justifications) to the PEC at the beginning of each financial year. Once the PEC has given its approval the views of British High Commissions and Embassies abroad are sought and they are asked in turn to seek the agreement of the developing country involved. This can be a very protracted process. Meanwhile a file search has been going on so that the detailed terms of reference can be drawn up defining the scope of the evaluation and the main aspects to be covered. The next stage is to choose the evaluators. The ODA usually selects mixed two-, three- or four-person teams, including one or two from inside ODA (or retired ODA officials) and the others from outside. The Department maintains a register of possible evaluators. If it is decided to go to a commercial consultancy (a fairly rare event because suitable evaluators can usually be found more economically elsewhere) the selection procedure will be supervised by ODA's Consultancies Section and will usually involve a tendering process. Increasingly the emphasis is being placed on the use of in-house staff (either from the Evaluation Department itself or from elsewhere in ODA on temporary release) although ODA usually likes to have an outsider on every evaluation to ensure a fresh and impartial viewpoint.

Before the team can go out to visit the project arrangements have to be made with the host country and they will be asked to nominate someone to participate in the evaluation. Unfortunately they often find this impossible, which is a pity because they have an important role to play in the evaluation process.

With the bigger evaluations the Department's usual practice is to set up a Steering Committee chaired by the Head of Department, which ensures that the interested parties in the ODA have a chance of making their views known on the kinds of issues to be evaluated. Occasionally it is thought desirable that ODA members of staff who have been directly involved in the project in the past should participate in the evaluation (eg because they may have special background knowledge or because the actual participation could be of special value to them in their work). In that case they are usually described as 'Assessors' and they do not participate in writing the report.

Once the report has been received the Department circulates copies to all those colleagues in ODA with a direct interest and asks for comments. These are then included in the cover note for submission of the project to the PEC. The cover note will contain the Department's suggestions on possible action that might be taken in the light of the evaluation, and PEC discussion usually focuses on these. It will also contain recommendations as to the confidentiality status of the report and any proposals for feedback.

2 Organising Feedback

This is the other main task of the Evaluation Department and it is the subject of Mr J. K. Wright's paper (Chapter A3).

3 Liaison with Evaluation Departments of other Aid Agencies

Evaluation is clearly an area where it is particularly valuable for there to be close liaison between aid agencies, because many of the lessons to be learned are equally applicable no matter what agency carries out the evaluation. This is most likely to apply to the lessons relating to the project itself, rather than to the administrative or 'aid delivery' aspects which could relate mainly to the way individual agencies operate: but even in the latter case there could be useful lessons to be shared.

The Development Assistance Committee (DAC) of the Organisation for Economic Cooperation and Development (OECD) took an early lead in this field by organising two conferences, hosted by the Netherlands, in the early 1970s. More recently the High-Level Meeting of OECD requested the DAC in 1979 and 1980 to report on the extent to which evaluations can throw light on the general effectiveness of aid, ie does aid work? The DAC responded by organising 'synthesis' studies of eight sectors, each member country being responsible for a sector (Britain was responsible for Rural Roads). The results were not altogether satisfactory, as the evaluations were not usually geared to answering general questions relating to aid effectiveness, but the High-Level Meeting gave the report a very warm welcome, as an honest attempt to answer very searching questions, and it approved a proposal to establish a DAC Expert Group on Aid Evaluation. This Group has met twice in Paris and has agreed a work programme which will have two main components:

a To continue the synthesis type of work, but this time relating it to a set of agreed issues rather than to sectors. These cover wider strategic and policy-oriented aspects as well as those related to specific projects and sectors b To share information and ideas on the development of evaluation work in the respective aid agencies.

To sum up, evaluation as a subject is rapidly developing its own corpus of knowledge and experience, and since it is by nature a process of learning and sharing there is a need to evolve ways and means of communicating the results to those who can profit from them. This was the main purpose of the Conference, and it lies behind the decision to publish these proceedings.

Discussion

Mr R. J. Berg (Overseas Development Council, Washington, USA) queried the accuracy of some of the estimates of how much donors were spending on evaluation. Increasingly donors were allocating funds for monitoring as part of the project funding, although the results were also intended to serve evaluation purposes. Total funds currently going into evaluation could be substantial and this raised the question of whether all this money was being spent in the interests primarily of the donor or of the recipient.

As to the staff of evaluation units, he said that experience in the United States Agency for International Development (USAID) had shown that the problems with projects in developing countries were seldom strictly technical in nature—they tended to be institutional and socio-cultural. If that were the general experience, it was important to have an interdisciplinary mix in evaluation work. He queried whether ODA's present Evaluation Department structure with its emphasis on economists was really adequate. Were the problems mainly economic ones? If so the structure was absolutely correct. But were not other problems at least equally important? If so a more interdisciplinary mix might be desirable.

Also on the staffing issue, Mr Berg queried the wisdom of ODA selecting only more mature people for evaluation work. He said that in his experience some of the really exciting evaluation work had come from bright aggressive people who tended to see things in a different way from older people. Surely there was scope for these, at least with project evaluation. (He recognised that for programme evaluation at the high policy level more mature people might be required). (The reader is referred to Mr J. K. Wright's contribution to the discussion in Chapter A3 for a further comment on this topic.)

Mr J. Jacobs (Freelance Consultant) commented on Mr Berg's point about the amount of money being spent on evaluation. He thought there were dangers in having a separate budget for evaluation work. The Swedes did it differently. They allocated one per cent of the budget of each project to cover the cost of the eventual evaluation. This might raise some problems, in that it was unlikely that every project could be evaluated, but at least it helped to ensure that budgetary provision for evaluation was assured. Unlike Mr Berg he did not think that it could be assumed that provision for evaluation was usually built into project funding.

Mr G. Schwab (International Labour Organisation (ILO), Geneva) wondered whether it was by accident or design that the word 'design' had not yet been mentioned! He asked to what extent ODA's evaluation programme was involved in the design aspects of projects. In response, *Dr Cracknell* agreed that possibly ODA did not interest itself enough in the 'design' aspects. This might be due to the influence of the economists who tended to lay greater stress on the cost–benefit aspects. Engineers for instance would be far more interested in the design of the projects. Perhaps this was an aspect that ODA should consider more closely.

Mr J. K. Wright (Under Secretary, ODA) said that, as Dr Cracknell had pointed out in his paper, evaluation in the ODA had its origins in the desire of economists to have a check on the effectiveness of the project appraisal techniques which had been developed during the 1960s and early 1970s. Before that date evaluation could not have been effectively carried out because the objectives were seldom properly specified, nor were the expected costs and benefits appraised in any detail, so evaluation developed as a means of checking whether the expectations at appraisal were being realised in practice.

Dr Cracknell said that although the economists had taken the lead in evaluation work, for the reasons given by Mr Wright, more and more ODA was moving towards the concept of a wider mix of disciplines. The problem was that with only 20–25 new evaluations to be carried out per annum it would hardly be possible to have an engineer, an agronomist or a medical expert attached permanently to the Department, whereas economics was a skill required for almost all evaluation work. When other skills were needed they were generally found from elsewhere in ODA or were brought in.

Mr W. A. Dodd (Chief Education Adviser, ODA) asked Dr Cracknell why, when evaluators had submitted their draft reports, the Evaluation Department sent back comments and initial reactions, with the suggestion that the authors might review their drafts in the light of these initial reactions. He wondered why ODA did not simply accept the draft report and cut out this further stage.

Responding, *Dr Cracknell* said that experience had shown that most evaluators welcomed the opportunity of getting some informal reaction to their drafts. Once the drafts had been submitted formally, as bound documents, they could not readily be altered, whereas sometimes a small factual error could ruin the impact of the whole report. On the other hand it was certainly not the intention of ODA to try to get the authors to change their minds. That would be to negate the purpose of the evaluation. ODA wanted evaluators to feel absolutely free to say what they wanted, even if they were things that ODA did not agree with.

Mr P. J. Wood (Commonwealth Forestry Institute (CFI), Oxford) suggested that, particularly from the recipient country's point of view, projects interacted with each other, often overlapped and were generally competing for the same resources. Therefore he wondered what could be done to ensure that the same evaluation was not carried out on overlapping projects. He asked what could be done to try to ensure that joint evaluations were carried out where projects overlapped between different donors.

In response, *Dr Cracknell* said that in practice there were not many such overlapping projects. Occasionally however, ODA had evaluated a project in which it was only one donor among several (one example was the Bosporus Bridge).

A2

The Work of the Projects and Evaluation Committee in ODA by Mr R. A. Browning, Deputy Secretary, ODA

ODA's main purpose in holding this Conference was to create an opportunity for an exchange of views between ourselves in ODA, and academics, consultants, evaluators of other agencies and representatives of the developing countries, on what is still a relatively new subject. I trust our decision to hold the Conference, and to publish the proceedings, will be taken as evidence of the importance that ODA attaches to evaluation. None of us can afford to ignore the lessons of the past, and if we are to avoid repeating our own mistakes we need a systematic way of learning these lessons and above all of applying them to our future work.

Evaluation is an important and valuable activity though some difficult judgements are required in determining how much of it should be done and precisely how to do it. The latter issue took up much of the time of the Conference.

Evaluation is used in ODA as a management tool to ensure systematic learning from experience. Its role must be understood in the context of an ODA system for trying to ensure that spending decisions are good ones and that decisions are implemented as well as possible. Thus we *appraise* before making decisions; we *monitor* the implementation of the project or programme we are supporting; we *audit* our systems internally (we are also, of course, subject to external audit by the Comptroller and Auditor General reporting to the Public Accounts Committee); and we *evaluate* the completed projects and programmes to see what we can learn systematically from experience. We think the system is a logical and coherent one and if feedback from evaluation and audit is well organised it can begin to look like a virtuous circle for self-improvement.

How much emphasis to put into each aspect of the system is a difficult matter for judgement. ODA has for long placed heavy emphasis on appraisal to ensure that spending decisions are well based. This continues to be crucial. In recent years we have placed much greater emphasis than previously on monitoring, on watching how things are developing and changing the shape of projects if things are not working out as planned. Resources, especially Civil Service manpower resources, are tightly constrained and choices of where to concentrate are difficult ones for senior management and line management within the ODA. Despite this we have in the last two or three years sharply increased the level of effort and resources we are putting into evaluation, though judging the right overall level is not easy.

The ODA has been doing evaluation work from as far back as the 1960s, but the subject really took off during the late 1970s. In 1979/80 ODA carried out seven evaluations at a cost of £50 688. A year later the number had risen to

12 at a cost of £140 861 and for 1982/3 the number was 19 at a cost of £279 560. The budget for 1983/4 is £325 000. This is rapid growth by any standards and it reflects both ODA's own appreciation of the value of evaluation activity and also the special concern on the part of various interested parties such as the House of Commons Select Committee on Overseas Aid and Development and the Public Accounts Committee. Britain has not been alone in this. There has indeed been a donor-wide quickening of interest in evaluation work in the last few years. The World Bank has established a high reputation for its evaluation work, and so also has the United States Agency for International Development (USAID) which originated the 'Logical Framework' approach. Other UN agencies and bilateral donors have now established evaluation departments and we were pleased to welcome so many of their representatives at the Conference.

The lynch-pin of ODA's evaluation work is the Projects and Evaluation Committee (PEC) of which I am the Chairman. The PEC scrutinises and approves ODA's policy towards evaluation and its work programme, as well as receiving all the reports on individual studies and recommending appropriate feedback arrangements. I will describe the role of the PEC more fully shortly, but first I would like to review the main objectives of evaluation work as we in the ODA see them:

a *To learn lessons from past aid activities,* ie so that we do not keep repeating any past mistakes. Evaluation is by no means confined to projects, it can also cover programme or sector aid, aid procedures such as briefing or recruitment of personnel, or indeed any activity that ODA (or in some cases the British Council) engages in. Since, unless they are applied, there is no point in learning lessons, feedback is a crucial part of evaluation, and Mr J. K. Wright takes up this theme in the next paper

b *To ensure as far as possible that the projects ODA funds have a good chance of being successful,* ie even though at the time of the evaluation the ODA has usually ceased to have a direct interest, we are still anxious that the project should overcome any teething troubles, and contribute to the country's development. Hence we try to conduct all our evaluations on a joint basis with the developing countries, and to help them to implement the findings. There is still a long way to go in enlisting the interest and participation of the less developed countries but it is certainly one of our objectives.

As important as evaluation in this context is the ODA's new emphasis on monitoring—which incidentally was due, at least in part, to the recommendations that were coming out of ODA's evaluation work. We see monitoring as the responsibility of those immediately in charge of the implementation of the project. It is important because it takes place at a time when it may still be possible to correct mistakes and to redesign the project to meet any unforeseen problems. Evaluation is carried out 'ex-post', by people not immediately concerned with project management, when it may often be too late to put things right. Evaluation tends to be more concerned with trying to improve the *next* project in a sector rather than the one being evaluated

c *To assure all those interested in development, not least the tax-paying public, that the funds used for overseas development are well spent.* Achieving this objective calls for a wide distribution of evaluation reports, but this can raise some difficult problems regarding the confidentiality of reports and these will be discussed later

d *To help those involved in the teaching of development studies.* The ODA has such people very much in mind when it decides whether or not to release the reports to a wider public.

It might be helpful if I were to describe the PEC's role in the evaluation process. The PEC is a high-level Committee comprising ODA's two Deputy Secretaries and a number of Under Secretaries. Its primary task is to advise the Minister on all substantial new spending proposals under ODA's bilateral aid programme. It meets approximately every three weeks. For some years now the PEC has been allocating a growing number of meetings each year to evaluation reports and the current pattern is that an evaluation meeting, dealing usually with about three evaluations, is held every six to eight weeks throughout the year.

The reports will have been circulated several weeks in advance under cover of a note by the Evaluation Department summarising the main findings and the recommendations, and suggesting appropriate action that the PEC may wish to take. Thus there is a certain amount of 'pre-digesting' by the Evaluation Department which facilitates the work of the Committee. Also the Evaluation Department will have canvassed the views of all the interested parties in ODA and its associated institutes on the evaluation and the gist of these will be conveyed in the cover note. At the meeting itself the key officials and advisers will be present as each evaluation is discussed.

The Committee is mainly concerned with the question 'What have we to learn from this project in terms of our aid procedures?' They have to assume that issues related to the particular kind of project or sector being evaluated have been noted by advisers and project officers—their main emphasis tends to be on aid procedures. The kinds of decisions the Committee takes could include: a revision to Office Procedure (an ODA internal manual), an addition to the ODA series of Policy Guidance Notes, a modification to one of the Sector Planning Manuals, or some change in ODA's internal staffing or operational systems. Ensuring that these recommendations are implemented is all part of 'feedback'. The fact that the same Committee as considers all major new projects also receives all the evaluation reports means that there is 'instant feedback' and the ODA has always considered this to be an important strength in its evaluation system. New arrangements are about to be introduced whereby when new projects are submitted to the PEC for approval the submission has to contain a statement that relevant evaluation material has been taken into account.

The Committee also has the key role of giving guidance to the Evaluation Department on the balance and thrust of its evaluation work. It does this formally once a year in February/March, when the Department submits its Annual Report and its proposed evaluation programme. The Committee checks that the evaluation programme is reasonably representative of the aid programme and it lays down the criteria for the selection of projects for evaluation.

But what can evaluation work achieve? Experience suggests that we cannot expect too much from it on the larger issues. Discussion among donor countries in the Organisation for Economic Cooperation and Development (OECD) suggest that, at least as at present conceived, the results will not answer fundamental broad questions such as 'Does aid result in development?' or even 'Would more aid lead to faster economic growth in developing countries as a group or individually?' What it can do, and is doing, is to show whether or not support for particular projects or programmes was justified in the light of their objectives; what elements of the aid delivery system could be improved and in what ways, and it can sometimes indicate more effective aid policies in particular sectors of developing countries.

Two final points:

a Evaluation of past experience has of course always been with us. Any responsible professional or administrator has looked as best he can at what past efforts suggest about future activities. However, it has not been done *systematically* and the emphasis at the Conference was on systematic evaluation and feedback

b Should we be encouraging developing countries to do much more evaluation of a systematic kind themselves, not, of course, simply of aid-funded activities, but of their experience in all sectors using all resources? While the answer might obviously be 'Yes', there must clearly be serious concern about how to ration the use of the limited skills and organisational and administrative capacities at their disposal.

To sum up, evaluation has become an important and much respected part of the work of ODA. The results are taken very seriously and they have had a significant impact throughout the work of the Administration. There is no doubt in my mind that we get value for money. Compared with a total aid programme of around £1000 million per annum, an evaluation budget of £325 000 (or nearer £500 000 if the value of ODA staff time on evaluation work is included), is not out of proportion. One only has to improve aid efficiency by 0.05 per cent to justify the cost, and we believe evaluation can achieve bigger increases in efficiency than this. But even so there is always room for improvement and we are looking forward to the opportunity for further dialogue that the publication of these proceedings presents; any ideas for improving our evaluation work in ODA will be considered carefully.

(Note: An expanded version of Mr Browning's paper has been published in the April issue of *Public Administration and Development* (Journal of the Royal Institute of Public Administration 1984) under the title 'Evaluation in the ODA—A View from the Inside'.)

Discussion

Mr T. P. O'Sullivan (T. P. O'Sullivan and Partners, Consulting Engineers) said that his 17 years of experience with ODA-funded projects had proved the importance of closer co-ordination and collaboration between ODA and consultants. This was particularly true with the new-style projects involving substantial technical co-operation, often in very low-income countries with only fledgeling civil services. He had certainly experienced the problem of a change of ODA desk officer having a great impact on the progress of a project (and no doubt ODA had also experienced the same thing with regard to consultants). Close collaboration between the consultant and the ODA desk officer was unfortunately the exception rather than the rule. One curious omission on the part of ODA was that it did not always ask for monthly reports (although consultants invariably produced these)—nor did it seem to be interested in improving the quality of the reports, ie in his opinion they should include more monitoring and evaluation information, and inputs and outputs should be quantified.

In response *Dr Cracknell (Head, Evaluation Department, ODA)* agreed that perhaps ODA had been remiss in not adequately bringing into its evaluation work the benefits from the increasing flow of data that was coming from monitoring. He said that monitoring was still fairly new in ODA and its potentialities as an input into evaluation work were only just being realised. It was important for instance that when the terms of reference for ODA monitoring missions were being drawn up the desirability of collecting data that would also be useful for the eventual evaluation should be borne in mind.

Mr J. Loup (French Ministry for Cooperation and Development) asked about the final stage of an evaluation before it went to the Projects and Evaluation Committee (PEC). He understood that a 'cover note' was produced by the Evaluation Department containing specific recommendations for action and he wanted to know whose responsibility it was to produce these recommendations. He was very concerned about this because his Ministry was at the stage where the newly formed Evaluation Department was just receiving its first reports and it had already become apparent that the consultants tended to be reluctant to make specific recommendations. This made it difficult for the Evaluation Department in turn to make specific recommendations to senior management—they did not feel well equipped to do this on their own account.

Responding, *Dr Cracknell* said that the ODA insisted on the evaluators making recommendations of a specific nature. ODA was not satisfied with general comments, however apt they might be, and evaluators were expected to get down to the specifics and not to be content with vague generalisations. One of the main reasons why ODA representatives were usually appointed to evaluation teams was that they could ensure that specific recommendations were made and that they were geared to ODA's operational requirements.

Mr J. Jacobs (Freelance Consultant) referred to the statement by Mr Browning that the Evaluation Department in ODA 'pre-digests' the evaluation reports in the form of a 'cover note' when it submits them to the PEC. He asked to what extent this process vitiated the whole argument that outside people were needed in evaluation teams to prevent the exercise from becoming too incestuous. He wondered if the Evaluation Department might sometimes be guilty of throwing out the baby with the bath water.

Responding on this point, *Mr Browning* agreed that this might be a danger. Indeed he had wondered when preparing his own paper, whether the fact that the PEC was both the progenitor and the consumer of the evaluations did not make the whole thing seem a little too 'cosy'. He was still uneasy on this score, but thought the really crucial point was that the members of the PEC should try to read the reports for themselves and not simply rely on the cover notes produced by the Evaluation Department: he thought that the majority of members of the Committee indeed tried to do this.

Mr D. R. Drabble (Commonwealth Development Corporation (CDC)) asked how ODA dealt with the delicate issue of the possible impact of evaluation results on the career prospects of the individuals involved, and for that matter on the re-engagement prospects of consultant firms who might have come under criticism. These issues could have an important bearing on the relationship between the Evaluation Department and the rest of the office, and between ODA and consultant firms.

In response *Mr J. K. Wright (Under Secretary, ODA)* said that as far as the PEC was concerned it had become the custom for any member to say, at the outset of an evaluation discussion, if they had been directly involved in the project although this would generally be known in any case. Each member was aware of the others' dark pasts, and this added relish to the discussions. As for other ODA staff who might have been involved, it was an invariable ODA rule that adverse comments would never be linked to named individuals in the evaluation reports.

A3

Feedback in the ODA
by Mr J. K. Wright, Under Secretary,
Economic Service, ODA

Evaluation without feedback is not operationally useful; the two make sense only together. There is little point in undertaking evaluations unless someone takes note of their findings and acts on them. But perhaps because there tends to be considerable pressure for the one (ie evaluation) and relatively little pressure for the other (ie feedback), or just because evaluation departments are often small and over-pressed so that there is not time to do both, feedback can easily be neglected. Evaluation is even seen sometimes as primarily a way of assuaging the doubts of third parties, rather than as an input and instrument for improving the efficiency of an aid agency. If that view is taken, then feedback is bound to suffer. If we recognise that feedback is an essential element in any useful evaluation system, we must also recognise that it has for many aid agencies caused the most difficulties. Setting up evaluation teams to carry out an agreed programme, balanced to meet agreed operational requirements, is a clear-cut task. But making sure the results of evaluations get back to the right people, and are used by them, is a more diffuse operation whose success cannot be assured by relatively simple administrative procedures.

I am far from convinced that we have yet solved this problem in ODA. What I have to offer is a number of reflections on how we see the task being carried out. I should say that 'collective amnesia' is not a weakness confined to aid agencies. It is widespread through government, and I would expect through the private sector too. In some cases, where the effects of loss of memory can be shown to be costly if not disastrous, care—sometimes elaborate care—is taken to institutionalise the collective memory. The military is a good example, where much thought and work goes forward regularly in order to produce, say, an Infantry Training Manual. There are other examples.

If evaluation work is to be effective it is essential that it be directed to problems as perceived by those trying to solve them in day-to-day work. This means that the programme of evaluation studies must be, and must be seen to be, directly concerned with the likely pattern of future work. There is in addition the problem of the form which a study takes. Is it likely to convince the desk officer that it is indeed directly relevant to his problems? One way we seek to ensure this is to use as members of the evaluation team officers from within ODA whose work has brought them face-to-face with the practical problems in the field they are investigating. In practice we have done this with good results; indeed the more knowledgeable the officer the more direct and astringent the report. Perhaps I should add that it remains a principle in evaluation that an officer does not evaluate his own past work.

To return to ODA's experience, in many ways the most important form of feedback occurs when the evaluation report is first submitted to higher authority and discussed. Much depends upon the kind of body that receives the reports. Does it operate at a senior enough level to be able to have influence on aid policies and procedures? Is it itself concerned directly with new projects so that it can ensure that the lessons from the evaluation are quickly applied to any new projects of a similar type that may be coming along?

In the ODA the same Committee, the Projects and Evaluation Committee (PEC), handles not only major new projects and major programme aid proposals, but also decides on the programme of evaluation work and has that work reported back to it directly. The burden of this in terms of the reports that have to be read is considerable (ODA's evaluations are usually detailed studies, and they can sometimes run to 150–200 pages, although it is now the invariable practice to include a detailed summary of not more than ten pages which contains the full gist of the report), but it is held to be justified in terms of the benefits from instant feedback. This consideration is one factor that explains why in ODA we have always tended to put a higher premium on quality than quantity. We feel that a few good 'impact' evaluations can give more useful and worthwhile results than a larger number of evaluations of the 'Project Completion Report' type can hope to do. These might be effective as a way of ensuring that funds have been used efficiently for the purpose intended, but only a longer-term study, showing the impact of the programme, can provide us with lessons of operational value.

However in this paper I want to focus more on other aspects of feedback because these are the ones that sometimes tend to be neglected. In the ODA we recognised back in 1982 that unless specific provision was made for feedback of these less obvious kinds it would probably not happen. So a Feedback Branch, with two economists, was created to implement a programme containing a number of components.

1 Early Warning System

One-page summaries of the highlights of evaluation reports are sent to all geographical desk officers who are handling new projects in the same or an associated field and to all ODA advisers. The 'EVSUM' summaries are accompanied by a note that alerts the desk officer to the existence of the full report and invites him to ask for a copy of it. It is the existence of this system that makes it reasonable that when new projects are submitted to the PEC for approval they should contain the now-required assurance that relevant evaluation material has been taken into account.

2 Briefing of PEC Members

It is one of the responsibilities of the Evaluation Department to brief the Chief Economist and myself on any evaluation findings, whether they be in the ODA's own evaluation reports or in those of other donors. The Department keeps an extensive and up-to-date library of evaluation reports issued by the International Bank for Reconstruction and Development (IBRD), the Asian Development Bank (ADB), the European Community (EC), the United States Agency for International Development (USAID) and other donors. This can be a time-consuming task but from time to time it throws up significant points from past experience that should be taken into account when new projects are being appraised (eg the experience of difficulties encountered by village people in maintaining diesel pumps has led to a reconsideration of schemes involving modern technology). This is one way of at least mitigating the effects of amnesia.

3 Syntheses

An important feedback activity of the Evaluation Department is to produce 'syntheses' covering the results of a number of evaluation studies in a particular sector. The idea is to look for patterns or recurrent features which, if they occur, enable us to have more confidence in deriving generalisations from evaluation work. One always has to remember that drawing lessons of a general nature from isolated evaluations can be a dangerous business, even if very experienced people can be relied upon to sense where general conclusions can be drawn and when they cannot. So far, syntheses have been produced for Roads (as part of a wider synthesis exercise organised by the Development Assistance Committee (DAC) of the Organisation for Economic Cooperation and Development (OECD), Programme Aid, and Hospitals, and syntheses are currently under preparation for Power and Irrigation. Sometimes an evaluation may cover a whole type of aid, or may embrace a clutch of projects so that it is more akin to a mini-synthesis. Examples are the recent evaluation of Programme Aid, comprising four separate country studies, and the current evaluation of the Aid and Trade Provision (ATP) scheme which covers a number of projects in three different sectors. During the past year half a dozen power projects have been evaluated and these will form the basis for the further syntheses studies mentioned above. A helpful feature of synthesis studies is that one can enlarge the coverage for any one sector by including the evaluations produced by other donors: obviously some of these other findings may be donor-specific but many will stem from the nature of the project or the sector, and this material can be as valuable to us as if we had assembled it ourselves. That is why in my view this should be a potentially fruitful area for inter-donor co-operation. The recent decision to set up a permanent Expert Group on Aid Evaluation at the DAC should open the door to further co-ordinated synthesis work (and indeed to several other aspects of co-ordinated feedback).

4 Amendments to 'Office Procedure' and 'Policy Guidance Notes'

One of the important ways in which the PEC ensures that the lessons from evaluation are incorporated into the ODA's procedures is through the office internal guidance manual known as 'Office Procedure'. This lays down the procedures to be adopted for all aspects of ODA's work, and it is under continuous revision.

Another useful mechanism, where the lessons relate more to broader concepts and cannot readily be translated into precise instructions, is the 'Policy Guidance Note'. Such notes usually run to a few pages and give general guidance on a wide range of issues. Evaluation results are only one contribution to these notes, which are based on the wide experience of ODA staff, but they certainly play a significant role. As examples, we have issued Policy Guidance Notes on Choosing between Consultants and Technical Co-operation Officers (TCOs), and on Programme and Sector Aid. The first of these was based on a study of the comparative cost of using consultants or

TCOs which was carried out by the Evaluation Unit (as it was then called) in 1979, and this was supplemented by ODA's general experience in order to produce guidance to bilateral programme managers about the considerations to be borne in mind when choosing between these two sources of technical skills for aid projects. The Programme Aid note provides guidance on the circumstances in which this form of aid is appropriate, its objectives, its design and appraisal, and the question of counterpart funds.

5 Training

An important channel for feedback is staff training. A number of seminars have been held in ODA based on evaluation findings, and sessions in ODA staff training courses have been devoted to the study of findings from evaluation reports. The evaluation reports are, where possible, made available to those who teach Development Studies, and to consultants or other experts who may be involved in development work. Unless there is a constant stream of results from evaluation flowing into the reservoir of training material available to the main training institutes, that material could all too easily become stagnant and lifeless. Evaluations make excellent case studies and are often used in that way.

6 Sector Manuals

These manuals are designed to encapsulate the experience over a number of years of people who have been dealing with a particular topic. They are more comprehensive than most other forms of feedback and draw on a wider range of experience.

They are used principally by economists and desk officers coming new to a subject they know little about. While they can, if they are properly assembled, give not only useful background analysis but also list the points of particular sensitivity, they are no substitute for help and advice from the full-time professionals in the field.

In practice, we have concentrated on writing manuals where there are problems in incorporating a new investment into an already existing system—where, that is, a discrete analysis would make little sense. We have written manuals on the Power Sector, Livestock and Railways and have virtually completed one on Roads. We are preparing manuals on Telecommunications and on Rural Water Supplies and we hope to see manuals on the Health sector and on other aspects of Agriculture.

These manuals therefore represent the last stage of feedback, the attempted synthesis of all relevant experience. While they are sometimes written by members of ODA, in every case care is taken to ensure that what is said accords with the views of a wide range of professional knowledge and experience outside ODA and indeed outside the country.

7 Feedback to the Less Developed Countries (ldcs)

This is probably the most important part of the process in the long run; it is also the part where we have registered least obvious success. Governments overseas are understandably interested, at least in the first stages, in being seen to be achieving results. This frequently means getting things built. But sufficient experience has been accumulated to convince us all that this is not enough; what is built or installed has to work, and has to keep on working if it is to produce the increases in income needed. It is by a systematic study of this past experience that the users themselves can improve on performance; evaluation should not be the concern only of the donors. This view is far from being generally accepted; there is still much to be done by way of recording and analysing experience systematically and so finding some way, on the spot, of ensuring that lessons once learned are not forgotten. Only some of the larger ldcs have as yet been engaged in evaluation work; Dr Shah's paper in Chapter C3 shows that India, for example, has established an evaluation system as comprehensive as anything I have been describing.

But India is an exception. Most other countries are only just setting out on this road and could usefully use guidance and training in the methodology and benefits of evaluation work. This topic figures later, so I will merely reiterate that ODA attaches considerable importance to it.

Conclusion

Evaluation without effective feedback is operationally useless. Monitoring the installation of a project is not enough; we need to know how well it is working, and if it is not, why not. We need to get these lessons thoroughly learned and passed back to the practitioners, both in the donor agencies and amongst the ldcs. Only if this is done systematically and continuously can we even begin to convince ourselves that we are near to making the maximum impact with the limited resources we have.

Discussion

Mr A. R. Ayazi (Chief, Evaluation Service, Food and Agriculture Organisation (FAO), Rome) agreed with Mr Wright that ensuring effective feedback was a very delicate and complex problem. But feedback based on what? That was the question. If it were based on a small sample of say only a dozen projects in a particular sector what inferences could be safely drawn? It was extremely dangerous to try to use the experience of a small number of projects for feedback purposes: one needed a representative coverage of different environments and conditions. Feedback had necessarily to be based on 'ex-post' evaluations because only these could yield useful information on the impact of the projects, ie only these could show whether the basic concept of the project had been correct, whether the organisational set-up had been appropriate, and whether the way the project had been implemented was valid in terms of the project environment.

Feedback had to distinguish between faults in the original design of the project and faults in its implementation. Most of the problems tended to be with the latter, ie you could take a good idea but still implement it badly. Feedback had to distinguish between these, and there had to be feedback to the project implementors as well as to the project formulators: to the recipients as well as to the donors. Indeed the most important form of feedback was to the developing countries, because the aid element might last only for a few years, after which it was finished, but the recipient was stuck with the project for a long time after that.

Mr M. L. Weiner (Director-General, Operations Evaluation, World Bank) also referred to the danger of basing feedback on the results of only a small number of evaluations. How did Mr Wright reconcile his statement that 'drawing lessons of a general nature from isolated evaluations can be a dangerous business' with the statement in the Evaluation Department's booklet *The Lessons of Experience* that 'the Evaluation Department is required to make specific recommendations for every evaluation report'?

Responding, *Dr Cracknell (Head, Evaluation Department, ODA)* agreed that it was dangerous to draw general inferences from small numbers of evaluations but he stressed that recommendations for follow-up action would only be made if the evaluation findings were confirmed by the corporate experience of colleagues within the office. He added that ODA was evaluating about one in four of its larger projects; but a much smaller proportion of the very much larger number of smaller projects.

Mr J. White (Organisation for Economic Cooperation and Development (OECD), Paris) commented that ODA's evaluation system appeared to be almost exclusively management-oriented, ie it was geared to things that ODA senior management were interested in. Thus the Evaluation Department selected projects for evaluation largely on the basis of the information needs of senior management. Feedback was also geared to this objective, and few other bilateral donors have so many means at their disposal for this purpose such as policy guidance notes, sector manuals and so on. However, as others had already commented, these lessons might be derived from a narrow base of experience. Evaluations in fact seem to be good at telling aid people how to do better in the future but they were not so good at telling them how well they had done in the past, ie there was a lack of real 'impact evaluation' that could yield reliable conclusions on an across-the-sector basis. He suggested that there was a tendency for evaluators to separate out the two things, ie accountability or performance on the one hand and what the whole story added up to on the other. The first was required for internal management purposes but the latter amounted almost to public relations. It was the latter that was generally given to parliamentarians to show that ODA had a splendid aid programme and that the money was well spent.

Mr White said that it puzzled him that evaluation in the ODA did not seem to be set up to provide senior management with a total picture of where the Administration had got so far. The World Bank had made an in-depth review of this kind (for example the International Development Association (IDA) Retrospective Study), and so had the Asian Development Bank (ADB) in its Task Force Report. Both of these attempted some synthesising of the general lessons across sectors. He argued that a synthesis approach at this level was more valuable for feedback than a selective pulling out of recommendations for doing things better.

In response, *Dr Cracknell* agreed that evaluation should be attempting to answer broad questions about the effectiveness of aid over whole sectors. He said that the Projects and Evaluation Committee (PEC) had begun to ask such questions and were requesting synthesis studies of the sort referred to by Mr White. The paper on Programme Aid prepared for the Conference was one such example and there were more in hand.

Mr D. McNeill (Development Planning Unit, University College, London) said that he had been commissioned by ODA to prepare a Sector Manual on Rural Water Supplies and he had been most impressed with some of the ODA evaluation reports with which he had been supplied, especially a major evaluation in Lesotho. If the water sector was anything to go by he thought evaluations of this calibre would make a very real contribution to ODA's knowledge of the sector.

He raised the question of whether there was feedback from evaluations into the terms of reference for future aid activities in the sector. His experience had been that terms of reference tended to lag far behind the current state of knowledge. He asked if there was any specific mechanism within ODA for ensuring that terms of reference were based on the experience derived from evaluation work.

Answering this point, *Dr Cracknell* said that the lessons of past evaluations were certainly being fed into the terms of reference for consultancies. The professional advisers were the main link in this. They played an important part in evaluations and they were always consulted in the drawing up of terms of reference. This was a very effective form of 'instant feedback'.

Dr D. N. F. Hall (Principal Fisheries Adviser, ODA) said that he had listened to his distinguished colleagues with some concern because as yet there had been little mention of the role of the professional advisers. He was not sure how to interpret this. It might mean that their role was so well known, and so highly valued, that it did not need amplifying, but it could be yet another indication of the erosion of the status and authority of the advisers in ODA that he thought had been taking place. They provided an invaluable element of continuity (he himself had served for 18 years as an ODA Fisheries Adviser) and often they were the only people who really knew what had happened to projects as recently as only five years ago. He was particularly alarmed by Mr Wright's reference to the sector manuals and sought an assurance that desk officers of the future would not think that they knew how to run a technical project simply because they had read the appropriate sector manual.

Mr J. K. Wright (Under Secretary, ODA) said that although feedback necessarily had to be a rather delicate matter outside ODA, within the organisation it could sometimes be pretty brutal. ODA had used some bright and knowledgeable younger staff to carry out desk evaluations based on a study of ODA files and the results had sometimes been very impressive. He suggested that there was nothing like putting a young Turk on to a job like that, ie to tear to pieces the work of his superiors. They usually did it with great gusto.

On Mr Weiner's point about the dangers of drawing generalisations from a small number of evaluations, Mr Wright thought this was possible without too great a risk provided common sense was used and the inferences were not stretched too far. It would seldom be possible to draw from an evaluation specific conclusions that would enable a previous course of action to be exactly replicated. You cannot find out from evaluation what to do on a battlefield, you can only take note of some of the things that are likely to go right or wrong.

On Mr White's point about the need for ODA to derive broad sector-wide guidance from its evaluations he sounded a note of caution. The variation in evaluation findings, even within the same sector, is such that it is often difficult to come to any satisfactory broad conclusions. As an example he quoted a recent exercise comparing the realised rates of return with those expected at the appraisal stage for a sample of projects. The results showed no obvious pattern, there were fertiliser plants with internal rates of return ranging from six per cent to 18 per cent per annum, and in small-scale agriculture the range was even wider from zero or negative to, in one case, 34 per cent. What broad retrospective conclusion could be drawn from such results? Perhaps only that one was likely to be faced with a wide range of possible outcomes and that this might be due as much as anything to variations in the quality of management. This was indeed a very important and delicate aspect of feedback.

Replying to Dr Hall's point about the ODA professional advisers, *Mr Wright* assured him that it certainly was not intended that the sector manuals should replace the professional advisers. They were merely intended to help a desk officer, or a professional adviser who was wrestling with a project in an unfamiliar sector, to at least find out what the pitfalls might be and to help him decide at what stage he should seek professional help from another ODA adviser or from an outside consultant, and then how he should formulate the terms of reference for obtaining that advice from outside the ODA. *Dr Cracknell* also stressed that ODA relied heavily on its professional advisers. They were always an integral part of all evaluation studies in their particular field and when the evaluations in which they had participated were presented to the PEC they were always present. Only if a specific evaluation's findings were confirmed by the corporate experience within ODA (especially that of the advisers) would the Evaluation Department feel confident in recommending that action should be taken. Evaluations were often used in ODA to bring to a focus various general impressions that had been gaining ground as part of ODA's normal process of self-examination.

Mr K. Winkel (Danish International Development Agency (DANIDA) Copenhagen) agreed with this observation and said that in DANIDA it was the practice to test the results and the recommendations arising out of evaluations against the corporate experience already existing in the Agency. He considered that a good deal of what was being learnt from evaluations was merely confirming the results of monitoring and ongoing evaluations.

A4

Some Practical Problems in Evaluation

(These notes were prepared by Dr B. E. Cracknell, Mr B. P. Thomson and Mr J. N. Stevens of ODA Evaluation Department)

A4a Conceptual and Methodological Aspects

1 The Objectives of Evaluation Work

The Comptroller and Auditor-General in his report on appropriation accounts for 1979/80 described the objectives of ODA's evaluation activities as 'to judge the extent to which the aims of aid have been achieved and whether there are any lessons which would contribute to the effectiveness of future aid'. These words were echoed by the Parliamentary Public Accounts Committee Report of 1980 which also referred to evaluation as 'a means of promoting the more effective and efficient use of aid funds'.

ODA's evaluation objectives can therefore be defined as:

a To assess the extent to which the aims of aid have been achieved

b To promote future effectiveness and efficiency.

In common with UN agencies and other major aid donors the ODA recognises three types of evaluation as follows:

a Evaluation of aid effectiveness: the extent to which a project's objectives have been achieved

b Evaluation of aid efficiency: whether those objectives were achieved at a reasonable cost in relation to the benefits

c Evaluation of aid impact: the wider impact of the project, ie in terms of the beneficiaries and its broader socio-economic and political implications.

a and b are usually carried out simultaneously.

The distinction between the evaluation of aid effectiveness/efficiency on the one hand and impact on the other is not always a clear one—usually the former will contain an element of the latter. Often it will be mainly a matter of the resources available for the evaluation and the timing of it (an impact evaluation is not feasible unless the project has been running for a reasonable time). The effectiveness/efficiency approach is the simpler one. It merely asks to what extent the immediate aims specified for the project or the aid activity have been achieved and what were the problems in trying to implement the project. All ODA's evaluations cover these aspects as a matter of course. The impact approach looks at the aid operation from a much broader viewpoint. It is concerned less with the achievement of the immediate objectives of the project than with the long-term goals. It looks at a specific aid project in the context of its impact on the whole community likely to be affected by it. In principle nearly all ODA evaluations are meant to cover impact aspects as well as the effectiveness/efficiency aspects but in practice the impact factors usually involve carrying out extensive field surveys and the true 'impact' component of many ODA evaluations is rather limited.

Different donors have varying approaches to the problem of deciding on the relative priority to be attached to these two objectives. The International Bank for Reconstruction and Development (IBRD) and the United States Agency for International Development (USAID) carry out effectiveness/ efficiency evaluations of every one of their projects but in-depth impact evaluations are confined to just a sample of selected projects. Because impact evaluations are still relatively few in number and cannot be considered by any means representative, they can seldom be used as conclusive evidence when one is trying to answer very broad questions such as 'Is aid in general effective?', ie 'Does aid work?' This is the question that the High-Level Meeting of the Development Assistance Committee (DAC) have been asking and evaluators have been trying to answer. The IBRD can point to the realised rates of return from evaluation studies but these are not (and cannot be) calculated for a wide range of socially-oriented projects, and even where they are calculated the methods used are not always entirely convincing, eg because they are carried out immediately the capital phase of a project is complete; the benefit side of the calculation is still almost wholly estimated. In the event the DAC evaluators had to reply that most of their evaluations were not geared to dealing with such broad issues and were usually designed to throw light on a narrower range of questions of the type 'Were the project objectives realised in an efficient way and were there useful lessons about the project itself, or about how the aid was administered, that might help improve future aid activities?' Nevertheless the wider question still remains and people will still continue to ask it. It is surely a reasonable objective of evaluation work to try to throw some light on these broader issues that have a bearing on aid strategies and policies. The DAC Expert Group on Aid Evaluation is continuing to look into these wider aspects.

It is worth noting that the developing countries are likely to have a different set of criteria from those of the donor countries when projects are being evaluated. For example, they may regard management weaknesses as an inescapable part of the learning process and they may put a higher value on the latter than the donor is likely to do. The donor may tend to ignore certain aspects of aid (eg aid tying) whereas the recipient will tend to attach considerable importance to them. Reconciling these different criteria in evaluation work may not be easy.

Yet another objective of evaluations is to learn useful information of a 'micro' sort about projects, eg crop yields achieved under field conditions, rates of build-up of traffic on improved roads etc, that can be applied in new project appraisals. Experience shows that unless these parameters are constantly reviewed in the light of experience they can become unrealistic and the appraisals based on them can yield false results.

USAID includes another objective which it has dubbed the 'antiprocrastination effect', ie the very act of evaluating a project (during its implementation) keeps the project managers on their toes. This would not normally apply to ODA's evaluations since they are usually carried out only after the projects have been completed and have had time to settle down.

2 Difference between Evaluation and Audit

Evaluation is not an 'audit' in the narrow sense of the word. Audits normally test compliance with management controls and regulations and they do not usually deal with the overall objectives set for an activity. To encourage co-operation in evaluation work ODA emphasises that evaluations are not intended to pin blame on particular individuals or organisations but to yield useful lessons for all concerned; hence evaluations are clearly distinguished from audits. Whether this is a distinction of substance or merely of definition is debatable. Some might argue that an efficiency audit is really very little different from an evaluation, and certainly the ODA's Evaluation Department keeps a close liaison with the Internal Audit Unit, but there seem to be dangers inherent in treating the two functions as if they were synonymous.

3 Methodological aspects

a 'Before and After' or 'With and Without'? An evaluation study should not always be merely a comparison between the current situation and the previous *status quo*. It may not be appropriate to make such a comparison because secular changes could have been taking place during the period, regardless of whether the project was there or not, and these changes should not be attributed to the project. To do so could be to present a false picture of the costs and benefits of the project. In these circumstances the evaluation has to look at the 'With and Without' position rather than the 'Before and After' position. This implies the need for a control group (see below).

b Need for a 'Control'. If the objective is to identify the benefits directly attributable to the project it may be necessary to set up a 'control' investigation, ie choose an area as nearly as possible identical to the project area so that the secular changes taking place during the period of the project can be monitored. This is by no means easy, but has been done for example with rural development and road evaluation where household and road traffic surveys have been carried out in areas similar in type to those served by the project but where no new developments have taken place. The problems about this approach are: the difficulty of finding suitable 'control' areas; the virtual doubling of the cost of the survey; the problem of explaining to the people in the 'control' why they are being interviewed without arousing false hopes; the fact that it often transpires that the changes wrought by the project being evaluated are in fact less significant than the whole range of secular changes that may be taking place at the same time; and simply the fact that this approach is only likely to be feasible if the evaluation is spread over a lengthy period of time, whereas most evaluations are one-off operations completed in a few weeks. The number of evaluations that have successfully made use of 'controls' is therefore limited, but we may have to use this technique more often if we are to measure achieved project benefits more accurately.

c How Important is it to Relate Achievement to Original Objectives? Most terms of reference require evaluators to work out the realised internal rate of return on the project and to compare this with the expected rate of return at the time of the appraisal. But this raises a number of issues. Is the objective to find out whether the appraisal techniques that were originally used were effective? If so presumably the rate of return should be recalculated using only those figures that could reasonably have been foreseen at the time of appraisal. But if the objective is to find out whether in fact the project is yielding a satisfactory return at the time of the evaluation one has to use the current data. Sometimes a project has a good internal rate of return but only because product prices have risen much more than expected or could reasonably have been foreseen, ie it has turned out to be a good project, but only because of good luck! *Vice versa*, there are evaluations that show the opposite, ie the project was well conceived according to the information available at the time but product prices have since collapsed (eg as happened with an ODA crumb rubber project in Sumatra) and it now shows a very poor rate of return. ODA does not spell out precisely how these problems should be tackled in its guidelines to evaluators but leaves it to the good sense of the evaluators to present all the relevant facts.

d How should Social Cost–Benefit Analysis be handled Ex-Post? All ODA project appraisals these days contain a social cost–benefit analysis of some kind, and most indicate whether a project can be expected to yield a positive net-present-value at the appropriate rate of discount. In arriving at these figures the economists have to make assumptions about the shadow price of labour, and where possible they apply the social cost–benefit analysis techniques as recommended in the ODA manual *Guide to the Economic Appraisal of Projects in Developing Countries* HMSO 1977. In addition where feasible they will attempt to indicate who the likely beneficiaries of the project will be.

The evaluator's task is to rework these figures with the advantage of hindsight—or to be exact *partial* hindsight, since the evaluation usually takes place only a few years after the completion of the project so that although the capital cost will be known, only the first few years of the benefit stream will be known. Evaluation therefore usually includes a sizeable element of appraisal.

Nevertheless the evaluator has available to him knowledge that the appraiser could not have had. He can find out, for instance, what the situation in the labour market has been since the commencement of the project, and can therefore work out the ex-post shadow price of labour. The results can be startling. For example in the evaluation of a phosphate project in Jordan the demand for labour in the Gulf States grew so much over the space of a few years that whereas a shadow price of 0.5 per cent of the cash wage was appropriate at the beginning, a few years later this had dropped to nil and there might even have been a case for a labour premium, at least for the more skilled staff. As yet we have very few examples of evaluations that apply social cost–benefit analysis techniques ex-post.

The same goes for the problem of identifying the beneficiaries of projects. This must necessarily be very much a guess at the time of the appraisal, but the evaluator should be in a position to carry out surveys and other investigations to throw light on this aspect. We now have a few evaluations which make a crude attempt to do this, but the difficulties are enormous as there are usually no data and unless field surveys were carried out as part of the project monitoring it is not usually possible to collect the data as part of the evaluation. Perhaps when we come to evaluate projects for which household surveys were carried out as baseline studies we will be in a better position, but as yet we are still very much in the dark on these distributional aspects. The IBRD has recently published a report on a very detailed study of the distribution of benefits in the large Muda Irrigation Project in Malaysia, which shows that the downstream benefits were much greater than had been expected. For example for every dollar's-worth of extra paddy rice produced there was another 0.75 cents in downstream benefits, eg in the form of construction work, transport, restaurants and other services, etc. Also the evaluation found that the increase in wages of the landless farm workers actually exceeded the increase in the incomes of the farmers on the project. This study shows how important the evaluation of the distribution of benefits can be, and we need more of such studies if we are to measure 'impact' effectively.

e Pros and Cons of the 'Logical Framework Approach'. This approach was developed by USAID and has been widely adopted by other bilateral and multilateral donors. The emphasis is placed on the proper identification of the objectives of the project right at the start—not just the immediate aims in terms of inputs and outputs but the long-run objectives and goals. Furthermore it calls for precise 'criteria of success' to be worked out at the appraisal stage (eg if it is an extension project the criteria of success might include x number of farmers contacted per year, y number of extension officers trained, and so on). Project managers then have to implement the project according to the objectives and the eventual evaluation focuses on the extent to which the objectives were achieved.

In ODA, we have never adopted the Logical Framework Approach in its full rigour, although we have always recognised the value of a clear statement of objectives at the appraisal stage. Our experience has been that a good project manager is someone who is all the time reviewing his objectives and if necessary making adjustments to the project if circumstances call for it. For example we funded a project in Indonesia for the production of cigar tobacco using sprinkler irrigation techniques. But almost as soon as the project started the price of cigar leaf fell drastically and the project manager wisely switched into sugar, oil palm and other crops. It quickly became a very different project from what had been envisaged originally, but rightly so. Under the Logical Framework system there is a risk that the process of adjustment might well have been delayed, to the detriment of the project. In our view it is not enough in evaluation work simply to find out whether the original project objectives were achieved: we have to look at the project in the light of the changing circumstances over the life of the project to date.

f Easily Overlooked Aspects. Evaluation can overlook or play down certain aspects of projects, just as appraisals can. For example ODA evaluations of fibre factories in Egypt and phosphates in Jordan both noted that the working conditions were extremely unpleasant and injurious to health. Unless the evaluation team includes people with the appropriate skills there is always a risk that the less obvious (but potentially important) aspects of this kind will be overlooked. Many of our evaluations have noted in passing that there were sociological and environmental aspects, but the evaluators did not feel well equipped to deal with these. When we did engage a rural sociologist to look at four ODA rural development projects he found that sociological issues had received insufficient attention and the projects had been weakened as a result. But to have a representative of every relevant skill on the evaluation team could be excessive and some assessment of priority often has to be made. On balance it would seem better to go for evaluations that are more comprehensive in coverage, even if this reduces the number that can be carried out with a reasonable allocation of resources, rather than going for a larger number and leaving significant aspects untouched.

Discussion

Mr R. J. Berg (Overseas Development Council, Washington) commented that most donor evaluation departments were ambivalent about the objectives of evaluation work. There were two schools of thought. One was that evaluation was to satisfy Parliament, and the other was that evaluation was part and parcel of good public administration, ie it was 'part of the package' of development assistance and therefore it was important that the developing country should be regarded as playing an integral role in the process and should eventually take it over. If the latter was indeed an important objective some different handling of the process and the products of evaluation by donors might be called for.

Mr J. K. Wright (Under Secretary, ODA) said that the resources available for evaluation were limited and therefore the one operation had to serve a number of different objectives, some specific to the donor and some related to the needs of the recipients. ODA used its evaluation budget to obtain management information that could both be of use to the recipients and also help in the British public relations context. On the latter point he stressed that public accountability was a serious matter and must always be an important objective of evaluation work.

Mr P. G. Rwelamira (African Development Bank (AfDB)) did not consider differing objectives to be a problem. In his view, assuming the evaluation was geared to evaluating a project as set out in the original appraisal report, whatever was contained in that report would be known to the recipient country and therefore (provided the evaluation was being carried out within that same framework) the recipient country should have no reason to object.

Responding, *Dr Cracknell (Head, Evaluation Department, ODA)* said that there had been only a fairly few instances where the developing countries had been reluctant to let adverse comments appear in evaluation reports for fear that this might damage their standing with the main aid donors. On the whole he agreed that most of them had an extremely relaxed attitude to the publication of the reports.

Mr D. Brewin (TETOC, British Council) said that one of the objectives of evaluations was surely to force those who had been responsible for identifying, formulating and implementing projects to review their concepts and ideas in the light of evaluation findings. He was speaking as a former victim of several of Mr Weiner's World Bank (very frank) evaluation reports which had hit him with the force of an Exocet missile. Anyone who had been involved with a project from the cradle onwards naturally thought of it as being his baby and when a missile hit the pram the effect could be devastating. But from this process something fresh was always learnt and this must be a main objective of evaluation.

Mr R. J. Berg pointed out that bilateral aid programmes suffered much more from the multiplicity of objectives than those of the multilateral aid agencies. He wondered whether one reason why the UK aid programme was spread over as many as 130 countries was that one objective of giving the aid was to 'show the flag' in a way that could not cause embarrassment. He suggested that a *de minimis* aid programme might have a completely different set of objectives from one that was aimed primarily at development. He wondered whether this factor had been allowed for in the ODA evaluations.

Mr R. A. Browning (Deputy Secretary, ODA) said that there was general agreement on how project evaluations should be carried out, and even on sector or programme aid evaluation, but as yet there was no clear understanding of how to set about evaluating what a donor's aid programme as a whole meant to a developing country. The World Bank's Colombia evaluation had highlighted the problems involved in trying to do this and the repercussions were still being felt. There was still a long way to go in these broader types of evaluation and maybe the most appropriate techniques still had to be worked out.

Mr J. White (Organisation for Economic Cooperation and Development (OECD), Paris) drew attention to the standard 'Glossary of Evaluation Terms' produced by the UN Joint Inspection Unit (JIU) in which a distinction was drawn between efficiency, effectiveness and impact. The first two were fairly straightforward studies of whether the project's objectives had been achieved, whereas impact studies were usually far more complex and involved studying all the implications of the changes brought about by the project. The classic examples of the latter were the many studies of the impact of the Green Revolution during the 1970s: these certainly showed that increased crop output had been obtained but they also drew attention to the importance of the associated socio-economic factors.

Dr Cracknell agreed with the terminology contained in the JIU Glossary but suggested that it was not always easy in practice to make a clear distinction between the effectiveness/efficiency factors and the impact factors. On one recent occasion, when ODA had commissioned a consultancy using this terminology in the terms of reference, the consultants had found it difficult to draw a clear distinction in practice. When did effectiveness/efficiency end and impact begin? If efficiency were related to the objectives of the project and the latter were set out comprehensively, would it not also cover the impact as well? Perhaps the distinction was more helpful in clarifying the underlying concepts involved than it was in a practical sense in drawing up terms of reference.

Mr W. Bor (Llewelyn-Davies Weeks and Partners, London) agreed that effectiveness and efficiency were obviously both important but he wondered whether they also covered another aspect which he called 'appropriateness'. By this he meant examining the terms of reference of the project and asking whether the most appropriate questions had been addressed in the first instance. It would be possible to go on evaluating against a set of wrong assumptions underlying the terms of reference. A project might fulfil the requirements of effectiveness and efficiency whilst still having the wrong (or at least inadequate) terms of reference and so be inappropriate to the particular situation. As an example he quoted the ODA's evaluation of the Bosporus Bridge. This showed that engineering-wise the bridge had been a great success, but the environment had not been properly taken into consideration. In short the terms of reference for the project for building the bridge had been too narrowly conceived. He was pleased to hear that ODA was now establishing multidisciplinary teams in order to cover a wider range of aspects which might not be immediately apparent if terms of reference were too narrowly conceived.

Dr Cracknell agreed completely with Mr Bor. There was no point in evaluating a project against the original objectives if they were clearly deficient. It was necessary to reassess the objectives contained in the original terms of reference to find out where they may have been inadequate or even misconceived.

Dr I. Carruthers (Wye College, Kent) asked whether the ODA was in practice carrying out the detailed procedures (such as shadow pricing, risk analysis and so on) laid down in the *Guidelines to Project Appraisal* and what light the evaluations were throwing on the effectiveness of these appraisal procedures. He asked if those who were involved in teaching Development Studies might have access to the evaluation results so that they could assess the implications of these evaluations for project appraisal procedures as set out in the ODA's Guidelines including the project check-lists.

Dr Cracknell said that ODA's appraisal procedures were constantly being reviewed in the light of evaluation results. As Mr Porter and Mr Wright were both members of the Projects and Evaluation Committee (PEC) there was instant feedback into ODA's economic techniques.

A4b Choice of Evaluators and Confidentiality of Reports

ODA has used a variety of evaluators, some from within the Evaluation Department or from elsewhere in ODA, some retired ODA officials, and some from right outside ODA. On the whole ODA's experience has been that a mixed team of evaluators (in-house plus outsiders) is likely to give the best results. The ODA staff understand the niceties of the aid relationship, and the intricacies of ODA's internal procedures, better than outsiders can be expected to do, but it is always good to bring in a fresh and impartial point of view. When ODA uses a mixed team it is usual to nominate the ODA participant as the team leader and he will usually take the lead responsibility for producing the report.

As to the choice of outside evaluators this will usually depend upon the nature of the project being evaluated, and the skills represented by the in-house members of the team. Sometimes a rather specialised skill may be needed that is not available in-house and so ODA has to go to a consultancy, sometimes a commercial firm or perhaps an individual consultant. Sometimes ODA is not so much concerned to find someone with a particular skill, as simply to find someone with wide experience who can bring to bear a non-ODA viewpoint. In such cases ODA tends to look to particular individuals on its 'Register of Potential Evaluators'. These are people who are felt to have the necessary experience, skill and maturity to make good evaluators—sometimes they will have been used previously and have built up a track record. At present ODA has about 150 names on the Register and there is a system of cross-classifying them in various ways, eg according to their areas of skill, the countries in which they have worked, and so on. Evaluation is a particular expertise in its own right and previous experience in the field is a distinct advantage. On the other hand ODA certainly does not want to repeatedly use the same small group of evaluators—it is important to bring in fresh blood all the time. ODA is therefore always interested in hearing from well-experienced, mature and qualified people who feel they have something to offer in this field, particularly if they have had a lot of overseas experience, and are particularly well qualified in one particular skill or area of expertise.

The question of the confidentiality of evaluation reports is indirectly related to the selection of evaluators because one way in which potential evaluators can improve their qualifications for doing this kind of work is by studying previous evaluation reports. This is one reason why ODA tries to make its reports available to those with a professional interest in the subject. Others who might fall into this category would include staff of universities, or Institutes of Development Studies, aid correspondents of papers and journals, other aid agencies in Britain or elsewhere, consultant firms who work on ODA-funded projects, and MPs or other individuals who may take a particular interest in aid and development issues.

There are however a number of problems to be overcome in making evaluation reports widely available. If they are to be useful to the ODA and the developing countries concerned, they must contain fresh and open assessments, and are bound to contain some critical comments. The basic principle is that evaluators should be instructed to write their reports 'for ODA eyes only'. The ODA checks that the reports contain nothing that might be unnecessarily offensive to the developing countries (care is taken to ensure that adverse comments cannot be attributable to named individuals—no one's career should be adversely affected as a result of their co-operation in an evaluation study), and then passes the report to them with the assurance that it will not be given a wider distribution without their agreement.

The Projects and Evaluation Committee (PEC) decides what the distribution of reports should be and it is naturally influenced by the content of the report. In some cases it may decide that publication would not be advisable. There are normally only a few cases of this type, so far not more than about 20 out of 200 or so. More frequently the PEC may decide that certain passages should be deleted. If this can be done without detriment to the main argument the report is then released for wider distribution. If it is difficult to alter certain passages without upsetting the balance of the report the PEC may decide that the report should be released only to people who have a precise and well-defined 'need to know'—an example might be a consultant firm engaged for ODA on a project to which the evaluation results are directly relevant.

In its recommendations for distribution of reports the Evaluation Department has adopted a liberal stance wherever possible and the PEC has mostly been able to accept their recommendations. ODA probably has as liberal a policy on the distribution of evaluation reports as most other aid agencies. This is in the interest of all parties. We all have much to learn.

Discussion

Mr J. White (Organisation for Economic Cooperation and Development (OECD), Paris) said that he was at first pleased when Dr Cracknell seemed to be advocating an open publication policy but had then been disappointed to find that this was only on condition that all the embarrassing bits were taken out. If this were done what would be the point of publishing at all? The Swedish Aid Agency (SIDA) had a different policy—some time ago it published an issue of its quarterly journal in which were collected all its horror stories, laid out for everyone to see! He could not see how evaluations could generate professional debate about how to make aid programmes more effective if all the embarrassing bits were eliminated.

Mr White went on to suggest that it should logically not be possible for a donor country to need to say rude things in its evaluations about the general deficiencies of developing countries (eg weaknesses in administrative capacity, lack of appropriate institutions, lack of budgetary resources for maintenance and so on) since these were generally well known at the appraisal stage and projects should have been designed to cope with them. Thus if deficiencies of that kind had contributed to the failure of a project that must axiomatically have been the fault of the donor agency.

Responding *Mr J. K. Wright (Under Secretary, ODA)* denied that ODA always eliminated the embarrassing bits of its evaluation reports: what was left out was anything that might be considered in a civil sense libellous and he felt there was every justification for that.

Nor did he agree with Mr White's second point, because many of the lessons learnt from evaluation studies went far beyond the kinds of generalities he mentioned—often one got down to fine points of detail. In a few cases ODA had had to decide not to publish some of the information in the evaluation reports, but that did not mean that it was not transmitted in ways that did not attract undue public attention. In matters of this kind one had to be discreet.

Mr P. G. Rwelamira (Africa Development Bank (AfDB)) did not see why a recipient country should be embarrassed by the publication of evaluation results. Admittedly if there had been financial embezzlement in the implementation of the project it might indeed be of some embarrassment to the recipient country, but really the problem (as Mr White had pointed out) must be with the donor country or agency since, if that had occurred, their investment procedures could not be very effective ones.

Mr J. Jacobs (Freelance Consultant) thought it was possible to 'offend without being offensive'. In other words there were times when ODA might have to risk offending a recipient country but this could still be done without being offensive. If ODA was not prepared to take this risk its evaluation work would be a waste of time. He went on to ask how in fact ODA got across the (presumably unpalatable) message of an evaluation in those happily rare cases when it had decided not to publish the evaluation report. Mr Wright had hinted at certain machinery that ODA used for this purpose. Perhaps he would elaborate on this. The recipient country was fully aware whenever an ODA team had evaluated a project so that possibly the most offensive thing ODA could do would be not to pass the report at all to the recipient.

In response, *Mr Wright* said that there was no precise machinery. What happened was that whenever an ODA official or professional adviser visited a developing country he would brief himself beforehand about any relevant evaluation reports and whilst there he would discuss in an informal but no less effective way the difficulties that may have arisen. All aid personnel were aware that they were part of a continuous and delicate relationship which should not be destroyed unnecessarily. Even if others might regard that as 'chickening out' that was still the way ODA had to do it.

A4c The Relationship between Monitoring and Evaluation

The main characteristic which distinguishes monitoring from evaluation is often timing. Monitoring generally occurs during implementation and its primary purpose is to aid the management of the implementation process itself. In contrast evaluation normally occurs after a project or a programme has been running some time and is primarily concerned with recording the lessons of experience in order to benefit other similar projects or programmes which may be designed in the future. The two activities are thus normally separated in time and also have different preoccupations: monitoring with a particular project's implementation and evaluation with its performance.

Of course it is often difficult to draw a precise line. For instance technical co-operation projects, such as an agricultural extension project, may be under implementation for a long period of time and monitoring and evaluation exercises could well overlap. Perhaps at the other end of the spectrum would be a discrete investment such as in a dam or a road where the monitoring would cease after construction has finished and the project has been completed but where evaluation would make sense only when operational data is available.

Nevertheless there is bound to be a relationship between monitoring and evaluation. Often the same data can be used for both exercises. Data gathered for eventual project evaluation (eg baseline data) can be used in project monitoring and vice versa. It is important to limit the data which is gathered to the minimum necessary for either the monitoring or the evaluation and to make as much use of common data as possible. Many projects have gathered far too much data which has neither been analysed during the project implementation, and so not been put to effective use, nor been amenable to incorporation in subsequent evaluations. So it is normally useful to design both the monitoring and the evaluation frameworks simultaneously so that they incorporate common data.

Too often monitoring concerns itself solely with the physical implementation of the project. However performance and effectiveness should also be covered. Monitoring should not just be concerned merely with such things as the rate of construction of buildings, the filling of posts, and the purchase of vehicles, ie with the expenditure of resources. It should also be concerned with the design of the project, and the continuing appropriateness of the objectives. There are many cases where proper attention to the effectiveness of project design during monitoring could have resulted in considerable improvements.

If the process of monitoring shows that serious problems are developing with a project it is often decided to carry out a special project review. Such a review is normally a fundamental re-examination of the project strategy and the use of resources during implementation. It is thus akin to a partial reappraisal or a partial evaluation. It might be thought of as being midway between the two.

The people responsible for monitoring and evaluation are normally different. Evaluation tends to be done by a team from outside the project management. The advantages of having an outside party to evaluate a project is that this should ensure a fresh and unbiased look. This is also so in the case of a project review. However monitoring is most often done either by a team from within the project management, or by personnel drawn from those responsible for the administration of the aid resources, if it is an aid project. However this has its disadvantages. Aid and project management is normally considered successful if it achieves the disbursement schedules on target. If there is no 'reward structure' for aid and project management achieving the physical targets in a cost-effective way this aspect may well be overlooked. It is probably inevitable that monitoring will be by the same people who are managing implementation; but if this is so then attention should be given to ensuring that project effectiveness receives suitable consideration.

One final common characteristic is that unless there is suitable feedback from monitoring and from evaluation to project implementation, whether it be the present project or future projects, then neither exercise will have been worthwhile.

Discussion

Mr G. Schwab (International Labour Organisation (ILO), Geneva) considered that the ODA definition of evaluation, as being related mainly to the timing of the activity (ie it was a process that took place after a project had been implemented whereas monitoring took place during implementation), was different from that used by most other aid organisations. It was more usual to define evaluation in terms of the nature and purpose of the operation itself rather than when it took place.

Mr R. A. Browning (Deputy Secretary, ODA) said that the ODA made a very clear distinction between monitoring and evaluation. Each project now had built into it, at the appraisal stage, the monitoring requirements, whereas previously ODA had assumed that regular monitoring would be carried out as a matter of commonsense even though in actual practice it had not worked out that way. The ODA saw monitoring as the process that took place during implementation, whereas evaluation was the process that took place after the implementation process had been completed. The main reason was simply the operational one, ie that it was the proper responsibility of project management to undertake its own monitoring. Some project managers in ODA, short of aid funds, had tried to transfer this responsibility to the Evaluation Department, but this in his view was most undesirable and that was why the Evaluation Department had been instructed not to concern itself with projects that were in the course of being implemented.

Dr Cracknell (Head, Evaluation Department, ODA) said that unlike the practice in the United States Agency for International Development (USAID) where evaluation was considered to begin with the statement of a project's objectives right at the start of the project's life and continued right through the 'ongoing' evaluation stage (which in his view was virtually indistinguishable from monitoring), ODA had decided that it was administratively more satisfactory to keep these stages distinct. There was always the risk that treating monitoring and evaluation as if they were virtually the same thing would simply confuse people and weaken lines of responsibility.

Mr J. K. Wright (Under Secretary, ODA) said he thought it would be quite wrong for the same people who were responsible for implementing projects to also be responsible for evaluating them—they were bound to be interested parties and were too close to the action to take a broad and impartial viewpoint.

Mr R. J. Berg (Overseas Development Council, Washington) suggested that rather than differentiate monitoring and evaluation on the basis of the timing of the exercise it was surely more satisfactory to concentrate on the different purposes of the two operations. Thus monitoring was concerned with the progress in the implementation of an aid activity whilst evaluation was concerned with the socio-economic results. Several kinds of aid programmes produced socio-economic results before the donor had declared the project to be at an end. Indeed the only definition he knew of the end of a project was when the money ran out from the point of view of the donor, but this was surely not a satisfactory basis of definition. For the developing country the project usually had a much longer life span. One could learn how to improve the socio-economic impact of a programme or a project before waiting for the donor to depart, and it might be important to do so. Monitoring usually had a very project-specific rationale, yet even so the lessons from monitoring could be aggregated and used for the transfer of important lessons into the corporate memory of the Agency just as were the results of evaluations. He would not be happy with a definition that regarded monitoring as somehow 'internal' and evaluation as 'external', because often evaluators were trying to educate the very people who were involved in carrying out programmes, and if one could educate them, for example to appreciate better the importance of checking on the more subtle socio-economic aspects of their activities as opposed to the straightforward monitoring of inputs and outputs, that would be valuable. In short he would favour definitions that would maximise the practical development effectiveness of the activities themselves both from the point of view of the donor and of the recipient (who might indeed wind up with yet different definitions again).

In response, *Dr Cracknell* agreed that the ODA was probably not making as much use of the results of monitoring missions for evaluation purposes as it should. There was as yet no adequate machinery in the ODA for ensuring that the findings of monitoring missions that could have a wider bearing on the aid administration as a whole were being fed back into the 'bloodstream' of the ODA.

Mr K. Winkel (Danish International Development Agency, (DANIDA), Copenhagen) agreed with those who felt it was unfortunate that ODA seemed to identify evaluation with 'ex-post'. He thought 'ongoing' evaluation was also very important. In fact DANIDA had decided to concentrate only on ongoing evaluations. He agreed that it was important to ensure that evaluation work had its own budget otherwise those responsible for monitoring might be tempted to eat into the resources available for evaluation. DANIDA ran about 35 major reviews and evaluations each year and he admitted that he had often found it difficult to decide what was evaluation and what was monitoring or review: however the more basic the questions being asked, and the more the original design of the project was being looked into, the more it looked like evaluation rather than monitoring. He thought ongoing evaluation was important because everything today seemed to be in a state of flux. He was afraid that if there was too much emphasis on evaluations by outside experts we might find ourselves preparing to 'fight the last war'. There were rapid switches in emphasis in aid strategies and virtually every two years a new aid policy came along. DANIDA's aim was to ensure that the experience being acquired was one hundred per cent relevant to the present and immediate future.

Mr I. H. McLean (Mackay and Schnellman Limited, London) also thought the sharp distinction between monitoring and evaluation was unrealistic. Monitoring was essential to management but it was also a necessary input to evaluation. If information was not monitored and recorded at the time it would be very difficult or impossible for evaluators (as he had found) to try to get hold of it eight or more years after the event. It became a piece of detective work, whereas if there had been proper monitoring the information would have been collected in a systematic way.

Responding, *Mr J. K. Wright (Under Secretary, ODA)* agreed that the recording of project information was a vital aspect of both monitoring and evaluation and the ODA frequently inserted a clause in project agreements requiring the recipient to provide the necessary management information needed for monitoring and evaluation.

Mr S. Maxwell (Research Fellow, Institute of Development Studies (IDS), University of Sussex) commented that throughout the Conference there seemed to have been too great an emphasis on the concept of a short evaluation mission. This was surely a misconception of what evaluation should be about. It was best viewed as a process that should start at the beginning of a project and continue right through, eventually perhaps throwing up a number of issues on which still further research would be required. Evaluation reports should not so much concentrate on specific outcomes (ie did the cement for the dam arrive on time?) as investigate the mechanisms. He had been working on the evaluation of food aid and the key issues were not so much whether the food actually arrived and was distributed but what effect the food had had on agricultural prices and the how and why of that impact. The facts in themselves were not the end-product, it was the explanations of those facts that mattered, but the necessary data was unlikely to be available unless arrangements had been made for it to be collected at the start of the project. There should be a model of the expected impact so that the necessary data to test impact could be collected as the project was implemented. The data requirements could quickly become enormous so what was needed was a simplified system of data collection for 'minimal monitoring'. The resources of money and people would have to be set aside for this purpose right from the start.

Mr R. J. Berg added a note of caution about overprecision on data requirements at the outset of a project. One could learn a lot from the un-anticipated results. For instance a classic case in America was a multi-billion dollar irrigation project in California which achieved its objectives of helping the California farmers, but at the same time it bankrupted enormous numbers of farmers in the Mid-West who received no subsidy. It would probably have been impossible to have anticipated this at the beginning. By tying monitoring and evaluation too rigidly to the objectives, as set out at the appraisal stage of a project, one might be militating against project evaluation of the unanticipated effects.

Mr L. P. Taylor (Selly Oak Colleges, Birmingham) made a similar point. He thought there was a danger in fixing quantitatively verifiable indicators of success of a project at the appraisal stage as was done in the Logical Framework approach because many of the changes associated with develop-ment were not in fact quantifiably measurable, eg the social, cultural and political aspects. He asked if the evaluations were going to systematically exclude such areas of change simply because the impact was difficult to measure in quantifiable terms . Would it not be better to search for ways of trying to assess such aspects more effectively? His own view was that at the end of the day evaluators could not avoid making judgements. He pointed out that the word 'value' lay at the heart of the word 'evaluation' and that all evaluations involved making value judgements. He suggested that ODA had already given some indication of its own system of values, ie it seemed to be evaluating aid projects from the narrow standpoint of more effective aid administration rather than from the viewpoint of the contribution of the projects to the total development process.

Ms M. Hageboeck (Division Chief, Programme Evaluation, United States Agency for International Development (USAID), Washington) spoke in defence of the quantification of objectives in the Logical Framework system. She said that it had never been the intention that these objectives and indicators should become a strait-jacket; the technique had originally been developed because at the time far too many projects had no clear objectives so that project staff had no clear idea what they were trying to achieve. The logical setting-out of the main objectives helped people to clarify their ideas about the project. The indicators of success were described as 'verifiable', but that was intended to include qualitative as well as quantitative measures. American academics had been arguing the relative merits of these two approaches for the last seven years but they had at last decided that both were equally necessary. She denied that evaluations concentrated only on the achievement of the specified objectives: they looked also at impact, unplanned and negative as well as other types of impact. She admitted however that some members of staff did not operate the system as intended—they did not use it as a way of opening up their thinking at the appraisal stage but simply tacked it on at the end of the process as an imposed requirement. Therefore the Agency was trying to bring the process forward so that the identification of objectives and verifiable indicators would inform the appraisal process from the very beginning.

Mr R. J. Berg agreed that qualitative tests were at least as important as quantitative ones. He quoted the case of 'rural roads' which had been the subject of an ODA synthesis. USAID experience had been that the internal rates of return on improving road surfaces were often low but if the local people were interviewed they were usually enthusiastic in their appreciation of the improved road—perhaps as much because, for people in remote areas, any sign of government concern for their problems was welcome. Qualitative aspects were undeniably important and one indicator of this was the fact that 350 000 copies of a recent publication on qualitative evaluation techniques had been sold.

Dr S. M. Shah (Planning Commission, India) said that evaluation necessarily involved both quantitative and qualitative material. For example, it was commonly stated that the Food for Work Programme in India had been a failure as it had not left behind any durable assets. When his Department set about evaluating the programme they had first to define the meaning of 'durable' and 'non-durable' assets and then they collected field data based on those definitions which demonstrated that substantial durable assets had indeed been created. An element of value judgement was involved, but even so a great deal of actual measurement was also required.

Mr J. Heidler (United Nations High Commission for Refugees (UNHCR), Geneva) asked what ODA's practice was in relation to programmes that might be continuous or for projects that might last a long time. Part way through the implementation period the donor agency might feel a need to take another look at the design of the activity or even to review the basic objectives. This obviously went beyond monitoring yet it could not be called 'ex-post' evaluation—presumably it might be termed a 'review'. He asked who in ODA would conduct such a 'review'.

In response, *Dr Cracknell* agreed that ongoing programmes (such as Books Aid, Training, Manpower, and so on) presented different kinds of problems. With these it was necessary to 'intervene' at some point and carry out an evaluation-type exercise. This was clearly not 'ex-post', and therefore ODA had tended to use the term 'review'. They were usually carried out by a mix of outside evaluators with people from within the Agency (either from the Evaluation Department or from the department responsible for implementing the activity).

Summing up the discussion on this topic, *Dr Cracknell* hoped that no one had got the impression that because ODA made a distinction between monitoring and evaluation it did not regard monitoring as of great importance. Indeed probably the ODA attached more importance to monitoring because it took place when something could still be done to improve the performance of the activity concerned.

A4d Criteria for Selection of Projects for Evaluation and the Role of Baseline Studies

1 Criteria for Selection

Those agencies that evaluate all their projects (eg the International Bank for Reconstruction and Development (IBRD)) do not need criteria for selecting projects for evaluation. However they were now beginning to carry out in-depth 'impact assessment' studies for a selected sample of projects and for that purpose they too needed some criteria of selection.

There has been a lot of debate over the emphasis that should be placed on the effectiveness/efficiency evaluation (typified by the IBRD Project Completion Report) compared with the in-depth impact-assessment type of evaluation. The former enables an agency to evaluate all its projects and this can be useful if it has to satisfy an outside body such as Congress in the case of the United States Agency for International Development (USAID), or the Board of Directors in the case of IBRD. But the latter, which usually involves independent evaluators, multidisciplinary teams and field surveys or missions, can yield more useful (and reliable) lessons.

The ODA currently evaluates only about one quarter of its own (significant) projects. Some UN agencies that have hitherto done only project completion reports are now considering doing a few impact-assessment evaluations experimentally. A few agencies are doing both.

Thus choosing criteria for the selection of projects for in-depth evaluation is already an important issue and is likely to become even more so as the relative importance of this type of evaluation increases. The ODA tries to ensure that its distribution of evaluations by sector, country, or type of aid does not get too much out of line, compared with the distribution of the aid programme generally. ODA has a particular emphasis now for instance on power projects and projects in India, because these had been under-represented in the evaluation programme over the previous five-year period. Subject to this general 'trimming of the sails', the other main criteria for selection are:

a Projects that are likely to be replicable

b Projects which are innovative or have a 'pioneer' element of some kind

c Projects which have run into particular difficulties and ODA needs to find out why

d Projects that are related to topical issues in aid policy or areas of increasing activity, eg the extent to which aid brings help to the poorest, cofinancing, or areas of particular commercial interest.

When the Evaluation Department invites the geographical desks to nominate projects for evaluation it asks them to state which of the criteria the project satisfies.

The process of selecting projects for evaluation obviously opens the door to the possibility of bias. Is there not a risk that only the better projects will be nominated? ODA's experience is that there is no evidence of systematic bias—any tendency to put forward good projects is probably counter-balanced by the fact that the criteria for selection include those projects that have run into particular difficulties. ODA finds that it gets a good cross-section of good and bad projects. The World Bank, and a few other agencies, evaluate all their projects and so they avoid the risk of bias, but there is a price to be paid since this absorbs such a high proportion of the resources available for evaluation that there is not much left for in-depth evaluations. On balance ODA believes a selective approach is necessary if the best use is to be made of the limited resources available.

2 Baseline Studies

A 'baseline study' is one that is carried out after a project has been approved for funding, but before work actually starts. It is designed to yield information that is not available from the appraisal document but which will be required if an effective evaluation is to be carried out when the project is completed. It should also yield results of value to the staff implementing the project, but insofar as the baseline study is initiated for evaluation purposes that is a secondary benefit. ODA has carried out baseline studies in such fields as rural water supplies (Swaziland), roads (Tanzania and Kenya) and rural develop-ment (Peru). These are all sectors where household or traffic surveys were required before the project was implemented if its impact was to be eventually evaluated with any precision.

The main problems are:

a Deciding whether a baseline study is essential; usually the information available in the appraisal is adequate. ODA only carries out such studies if there is a very strong case

b Baseline studies can pre-empt available funds that may be needed for evaluations, and the benefit may not be realised for some years ahead

c Should the baseline survey concentrate on surveys of individual households with the objective of going back to those same households when the time comes to do the evaluation? Or should it be accepted that households change so much over a period of years that it is better to work on a representative sample basis? So far ODA has tended to do both as one cannot be sure which technique will prove most useful

d Should one aim for the same people who carried out the baseline to go back later to do the evaluation? ODA sees considerable advantages in this, not least that they are likely to get better co-operation in carrying out the household surveys as they will be familiar to the people being interviewed. Often however it will not be feasible to arrange this because of the lapse of time.

View of the Institute of Development Studies at the University of Sussex, Falmer, Brighton.

Mr R. A. Browning, Deputy Secretary, ODA, giving the Opening Address.

Discussion

Mr J. Jacobs (Freelance Consultant) pointed out that whereas provision was built into projects for monitoring during implementation apparently no provision was made for baseline studies that might be required if an effective evaluation was eventually to be possible. *Mr R. A. Browning (Deputy Secretary, ODA)* said that, if necessary, arrangements were made for baseline studies to be carried out if it was clear that this data would be needed. This could be important to some projects but certainly not for all. *Dr Cracknell (Head, Evaluation Department, ODA)* said that it was unnecessary to make specific provision for baseline studies as part of the project funding because the ODA had set aside an annual budget for evaluation work and this covered the requirements for baseline studies.

Mr F. G. Holder (United Nations/Food and Agriculture Organisation (UN/FAO) World Food Programme (WFP), Rome) wondered if it was absolutely necessary to set up expensive baseline surveys using expatriate teams. An alternative would be to ensure that the main data requirements for monitoring and evaluation were carefully specified at the outset by the desk officer, the people who would carry out the monitoring and the evaluation department. WFP experience had been that if enough attention was devoted to this and the right data selected the project manager could be trusted to ensure that the information was in fact collected. A lot more work is needed to be done in simplifying the data requirements and making sure that everyone agreed with the format and the selection of data to be collected. The project manager should be entrusted with this responsibility right from the beginning.

Dr R. M. Lawson (Consultant Fisheries Economist, Centre for Fisheries Studies, Humberside College of Higher Education) referred to the problems she had had in establishing a baseline for the evaluation of fisheries projects in Kiribati for ODA. These projects dated back to 1970, to a time when the economy was extremely undeveloped and there was little or no concept of private property. The ODA files had no baseline data and she would have had great difficulties had it not been for the fortunate chance that the ODA Principal Fisheries Adviser came up with a report from the late 1960s by a New Zealand university which contained invaluable anthropological information. If it was not possible to get a specific baseline studies done, at least the ODA desk officer should be on the lookout for useful socio-economic data and research reports that might serve a similar purpose. She added that many developing countries were eager to invest in fisheries projects, not only for economic reasons but also to further political, strategic or even military objectives. It was difficult to evaluate one specific project without looking at developments in the fisheries sector as a whole. She referred to the work of the FAO in compiling data on aid to fisheries in general and she wondered if ODA could do something similar.

Professor D. Colman (University of Manchester) suggested that the concept of baseline studies would have to be broadened if there was to be any hope of effectively identifying the beneficiaries of the projects. Thus with a rural development project for example, the baseline study would need to identify the dynamics of the smallholder sector by means of a simple model which could incorporate some kind of structural understanding of the system so that the beneficiaries could be identified. Even this might not succeed and it could be that evaluators were deluding themselves if they thought that the beneficiaries could be identified with any precision.

A4e The Role of the Less Developed Countries (ldcs) in Evaluation Work

The subject of evaluation ought to be of interest to ldc governments both from the point of view of the future management of the projects being evaluated, and also because they need to evaluate their own investments. For this reason ODA now tries whenever possible to carry out its evaluations on a joint basis with the ldcs and several such evaluations are currently underway.

Even when ldc governments do not have the capacity to provide evaluators, co-operation with them is still important if the evaluation is to be a success. In any event a donor cannot visit projects overseas unless the government gives its permission. This in our experience is rarely withheld, although delays can sometimes occur at this stage.

The feedback of evaluation results to ldcs and getting their reactions to them is most important, but there are some difficulties. ODA now usually sends the final reports to ldc governments, but so far they have not been invited to comment formally, nor have they usually been much involved in the preparation of the draft reports. If the ldc's government has not participated in the evaluation there will be no one in the ldc who feels any responsibility for the report; human nature being what it is the report may well languish unnoticed and without influence. ODA is now considering sending at least some evaluators back to ldcs to discuss the report findings with ldc officials.

Evaluation ought not to be just a donor activity. ODA was pleased to welcome at the Conference a representative of the Indian Government Evaluation Service, and his paper showed that in India at least evaluation is a major activity. ODA has tried to encourage self-help evaluation work by the ldcs themselves and has financed such work in Swaziland, Malawi and Indonesia. Training is another area where ODA willingly assists when requested. A course in evaluation techniques has been successfully established at the University of East Anglia.

Discussion

Mr J. Jacobs (Freelance Consultant) observed from recent experience in evaluation work in Uganda that the problem was not so much that ldc staff were not available to participate in evaluation teams but that they were generally reluctant to play this role for fear that it would require them to be critical of local people responsible for the implementation of the project. He asked if it could not be a prerequisite of an evaluation that there should be some active participation in it by local people. *Dr Cracknell (Head, Evaluation Department, ODA)* agreed that people from developing countries were seldom prepared to be critical of their own countrymen. In the few instances where ODA had arranged for someone from a developing country to be attached to an evaluation team the problem had been circumvented by a form of words which acknowledged that person's contribution, but made it clear that he was in no way associated with the findings. One of ODA's firm rules was that evaluation reports should never contain derogatory remarks about named individuals, whether in Britain or overseas.

Mr J. N. Stevens (Evaluation Department, ODA) said that Mr Weiner's paper (Chapter C1) contained the interesting suggestion that the developing countries should be encouraged to prepare project completion reports as a first step in encouraging the development of their own evaluation skills and capabilities. He would be interested to hear the views of other participants on this suggestion. He also commented on the suggestion in Dr Shah's paper that the donor countries should make better use of developing country experts as evaluators. He said the ODA recognised the importance of this, and indeed had set up joint evaluations with the Indian Government but there were difficulties in this approach so long as British aid funds were tied to the use of British consultants.

Mr F. G. Holder (United Nations/Food and Agriculture Organisation (UN/FAO) World Food Programme (WFP), Rome) referred to the problem of the small numbers of professional staff in the recipient countries capable of carrying out review or evaluation work, so that if they were pressed to participate in donor evaluations this would mean diverting staff from more essential work. The FAO did not have the resources to train evaluators in the recipient countries. He said that joint missions were uncommon as it was thought that this could affect the impartiality of the reports. It was not all that difficult to get developing country staff to be associated with evaluation missions, but they would seldom be prepared to sign the report or to have their names linked with it. The WFP always agreed the terms of reference with developing country governments: it always incorporated data requirements for monitoring and evaluation in the original terms of reference; and it always requested the developing countries to appoint observers to accompany their missions. Thus the developing countries were fully aware of all that went on, but they were under no pressure to sign any document at the end of the day. The participation of observers was a useful training exercise and it also meant that there was usually no difficulty about including criticisms in the reports because the observers had seen the problems for themselves and could hardly disagree. Moreover there was more chance of the recommendations being implemented. Finally, many senior administrators in the developing countries were tied by pressure of work to their desks: it was one of the benefits of evaluation missions that they sometimes gave these administrators the much needed opportunity to get out and see things for themselves. Conversations under a tree in a village, or at night in the bar, were all a valuable part of the training and exchange of ideas that evaluation work made possible.

Mr A. R. Ayazi (Chief, Evaluation Service, FAO, Rome), having previously ascertained from Mr Stevens that ODA does not specifically instruct its evaluation teams to brief developing country officials on its findings before it leaves (ie ODA leaves that to their discretion), said that in the UN agencies the rules on this were quite definite. Each evaluation mission was instructed to brief the developing country officials (and also the UN agencies in that country) on its results. This enabled any factual errors to be corrected and gave an opportunity for last minute additions to the coverage of the evaluation if that were deemed necessary.

Responding to Mr Stevens' comment on the project completion reports he thought these could be very useful although he was not sure that they could be entirely left to the developing countries. Project completion reports should be prepared as a joint activity between the donor country (or agency) and the recipient. In practice most United Nations project completion reports were written by the agency staff and that was unfortunate. He wanted to see the project completion reports more 'evaluation oriented' with less emphasis on mere facts and more on the impact of the project.

As to monitoring by the developing countries Mr Ayazi said that FAO was finding it very difficult, particularly in the least developed countries (lldcs), to get complex monitoring systems established. It was essential to simplify the systems and to concentrate on just the results that were needed to form judgements. He said that little had been done to promote training in monitoring and evaluation and this was something all donors should promote following the lead given by the World Bank. Donors should also do their best to build up and strengthen the institutions in developing countries that were responsible for monitoring and evaluation: large capital aid projects should all have built into them monitoring and evaluation units.

Mr K. Winkel (Head, Evaluation Unit, Danish International Development Agency (DANIDA), Copenhagen) said that DANIDA had found it easier to arrange developing country participation in ongoing evaluations than in ex-post evaluations. He quoted two examples. The first was a £15 million health and family welfare project in India for which a ten-man monitoring and evaluation team had been established (three Danish, seven Indian). This was proving highly effective and was also performing a very useful training function. The second example was an integrated rural development programme in the Noakhali District of Bangladesh. The Danish contribution was £10 million and there was a monitoring and evaluation team comprising one Dane and 12 Bangladeshis all of whom had been trained in the techniques. This approach was probably the best way to train the developing countries in monitoring and evaluation methods. It may be that in ten years' time an ex-post evaluation might be feasible, but the main aim at present was to fully involve the local people in project monitoring and evaluation as an ongoing exercise.

Ms M. Hageboeck (Division Chief, Programme Evaluation, United States Agency for International Development (USAID), Washington) thought that it was not enough merely to arrange for developing country participation in monitoring and evaluation work. The evaluation reports would probably lie unused on the developing country's shelves. The problem was how to ensure that effective action was taken based on the evaluation findings and that was just as much a problem in the developing countries as it was for the donors.

Mr J. Jacobs took up the same theme. He felt there had been a shadow overhanging the proceedings throughout the day and that was the ODA's admission that it had made little progress in encouraging the developing countries to improve their own evaluation capability. He had recently been trying to persuade a developing country to reduce the number of its ministries and administrative departments by half but had been unsuccessful because they had no capacity to appreciate cost–benefit analysis. If participation in monitoring and evaluation work were capable of enhancing their capabilities in that direction that would be a valuable spin-off benefit.

Mr L. P. Taylor (Selly Oak Colleges, Birmingham) suggested that aid donors should be prepared to submit their own policies and procedures to evaluation by the recipients as the Dutch voluntary aid agency, Inter-Church Co-ordinating Committee for Development Projects (ICO) had already done.

Mr M. L. Weiner (Director-General, Operations Evaluation, World Bank) agreed but pointed out that there was a fundamental distinction between bilateral and multilateral agencies in this regard. The recipient countries were part owners of the multilateral agencies even though they might not feel that they were or indeed behave as if they were. Nonetheless they had a voice on the governing boards and they had some influence. He described the bank's procedures for eliciting the views of recipient countries on evaluation reports. Every draft report was sent to the recipient and their comments were invited. These were then annexed to the reports. Unfortunately there was an almost total lack of stimulating comment; however, it was hardly surprising that a recipient country should be reluctant to speak harshly of a donor with whom it wished to preserve a harmonious relationship. If there were harsh comments to be made other means would generally be found. Thus in reality this was a complex situation but all the same he felt that attempts to involve the recipient countries fully must continue to be made.

Mr R. J. Berg (Overseas Development Council, Washington) said that he felt strongly about the importance of the role of the developing countries in evaluation because he suspected that they would define the issues in a way more relevant for development than the donors tend to do. There might be say 17 aid donors engaged in an activity, each of which saw only its own part, but the developing country would naturally see the whole as one activity. They would want to evaluate not just one donor contribution but the activity as a whole. *Dr I. Carruthers (Wye College, University of London)* asked Mr Berg why he thought the developing countries might frame the important questions in a more development-minded way than the representatives of the donor countries, when recent studies had indicated that it was in fact to the capital cities of the developing countries that a lot of the impediments to development could be traced. *Mr Berg* said he certainly did not intend to disparage the excellent contributions made by the donor countries, but he was concerned that each donor was interested in evaluating its own contribution to an institution or a project rather than the institution or project as a whole. For example he had seen too many instances of a university campus in a developing country where each donor independently would be evaluating (and at different times) its own specific contribution to this or that building, whereas what the university authorities were really interested in was how effectively the institution as a whole was operating.

Mr R. A. Browning (Deputy Secretary, ODA) doubted if the aid donors would ever be willing to collaborate in the way Mr Berg seemed to envisage. Most bilateral donors were motivated by factors that were not wholly developmental: historical, traditional and other links also played an important part. Each donor might be prepared to inform the others of what it was doing, but he could not foresee much closer collaboration than that. He asked Dr Shah if he could say, from the basis of his own experience as an evaluator, what he thought had been the impact of aid on India and how aid was being administered. *Dr S. M. Shah (Planning Commission, India)* replied that aid funds had not been accounted for separately in the Indian planning system so that in effect they became absorbed into the total Indian programme.

PART

SOME KEY FINDINGS FROM ODA EVALUATIONS IN SELECTED SECTORS

B1

Natural Resources by Dr G. D. Gwyer, Mr J. C. H. Morris and other natural resources economists in ODA

Introduction

The objective of this paper is to review 21 evaluations that ODA has carried out in the Natural Resources Sector and to see what lessons have emerged and what changes ODA has made in the light of them.

Natural resources covers a wide field. It includes rural development projects in general as well as projects specifically related to agriculture, forestry or fishery. Agriculture can be subdivided into major sub-sectors such as irrigation, livestock, farm power and commodities. ODA has only evaluated two or three projects in each sub-sector so that trying to draw general inferences from such a limited stock of raw material can be a hazardous enterprise. What this paper does is to identify the main lessons that have emerged from the evaluations and then to cross-check them against ODA's wider experience generally and against other published work in the field. The aim is to show how ODA's policies and procedures in this sector have been responsive to the broad array of evidence as to aid-effectiveness, of which evaluation is only a part.

Results from some ODA evaluations

In the natural resources field, the evaluation studies have been grouped as follows:

    integrated rural development projects
    irrigation projects
    farm power projects
    commodity programmes
    fisheries projects
    forestry projects
    livestock projects.

Each of these categories is discussed in turn.

As a result of ODA's strategy of increased aid to the poorest, increased efforts were made during the mid-1970s to identify and finance projects in the rural sector that would have the desired impact on the poorer members of society. One of the main vehicles for bringing about increased aid to the rural sector were the Integrated Rural Development Projects (IRDPs). These projects were seen to offer the opportunity to enable a major thrust to be made on improving the incomes and standard of life of as broad a mass of people as possible. They were generally carried out in the poorest parts of a particular country so that the objectives of the new strategy could be realised. They were usually multisector and multicomponent.

ODA's main experience lies in Africa where it has jointly funded several projects with the International Bank for Reconstruction and Development (IBRD). These projects have been reviewed by Mr J. C. H. Morris in an unpublished paper entitled 'A Synopsis of Reviews of Six African Rural Development Projects', November 1981. Included in the Synopsis is an ODA evaluation of the 'South Darfur Rural Development Project, Sudan'.* The conclusions which emerge from this overview were that the projects were not necessarily failures but that some aspects of their design and preparation had been shown during their implementation to indicate some general weaknesses as follows:

a They were based upon insufficient knowledge of existing farm systems

b More on-farm testing of the proposed crop production technology was required

c Assumptions on the rate of adoption of new agricultural technology were considerably over-optimistic

d There were deficiencies in analysing and valuing increased farm labour inputs; in particular, unrealistically low opportunity costs of labour were used, ignoring alternative farm and off-farm income opportunities

e Project proposals were not sufficiently financially attractive to farmers

f Market and price policies were inconsistent with project objectives

g There existed an inhospitable economic situation

h The project management was overburdened due to complex multisector project design

i Project management was too divorced from existing institutions

j More consideration should have been given to sociological constraints

k There was a need for more effective monitoring.

In addition to Morris's reviews, P. Devitt completed an ODA evaluation in November 1978 which also served to demonstrate problems from other ODA rural development projects in Africa ('The Role of Sociological Factors in four ODM Projects'). The main conclusion of the evaluation was that sociologists should be involved in development project pre-implementation phases, and during the project, to enable a better understanding of the systems and to detect any 'unintended consequences that may have arisen'.

Sociologists now have a much more important role in ODA project appraisal. However, there still remain problems in providing a sociological input as traditionally, agricultural, engineering and economic advisers have held sway in project appraisal and design and their role is easier to grasp than that of the sociologist.

The ODA's experience of IRDPs in Asia is more limited, with only the Kosi Hills Area Rural Development Programme (KHARDEP) Project in Nepal qualifying as an IRDP. A mid-term review was carried out in mid-1982 by a team of ODA and Nepal government officials but there has been no formal evaluation. Even though the Asian experience is more complex due to the greater social differentiation, the issues raised on connection with African projects apply, although the conclusions have a somewhat different emphasis.

---

*A bibliography starts on page 61.

In particular, poverty-oriented projects tend to deal with a particular grouping (eg the marginal farmer) within an area rather than a geographical approach as is embodied in the IRDP concept. Moreover, in Asia, a knowledge of crop production technology in irrigated areas is not usually a major problem. Similarly, the returns to farm labour are a less important issue usually than the returns to land.

As a result of these evaluations and reviews, ODA has modified its approach to IRDP appraisal and strategies in general for rural development. The main features are:

a There should be more emphasis on agricultural research. Such research should be oriented to producing improved financial returns to smallholder labour and attention should be given to mixed cropping systems particularly in rainfed and semi-arid areas

b Technical and adaptive research should be closely co-ordinated with research into the socio-economic features since agronomically sound packages have so often failed for these reasons in the past. This conclusion, of course, is consistent with the new emphasis on the Farm Systems Research approach

c Project appraisal should either be based on a farming system that is known to be attractive to the small farmer or else the project should incorporate in the initial stages adaptive research work on the lines outlined above. The essential point is to develop whole or partial packages that are financially attractive to the farmer and are applicable to his or her existing social and environmental conditions. A technically sound financial viability analysis of the whole farm, properly incorporating a full cost of production budget with an inputed value for the opportunity cost of any change in farm labour input, is invariably required

d For these reasons, and in view of the time required to produce sufficiently firm results, a pilot phase is often advisable to demonstrate project feasibility or to develop a viable project strategy. Such a phase would also provide the opportunity to identify deficiencies in input supply, marketing and price policies which can jeopardise the success or otherwise of well-designed projects

e There is a need for less complex projects, with a greater use of phased programmes covering a longer time frame than the typical three-to-five-year project

f Attention should be paid to the balance between directly productive activities and those which are less directly productive (eg health, infrastructure). A proliferation of activities makes projects too complex to manage effectively and it is therefore necessary to concentrate on initial constraints and discard in the short term desirable, but less productive, activities. Ultimately substantial expenditures on the 'social services' elements such as health or roads and requiring recurrent expenditure substantially in excess of levels in other areas of the country, may not be sustainable in the long term unless the productive element is successful, or unless recurrent finance is available for redistribution from other productive sectors of the economy g In general, it is preferable to build on existing institutions than to create new ones. This can sometimes be more difficult in the short-term but can give longer-term benefits

h Project monitoring should include monitoring of the agricultural results and provide effective feedback on project implementation directly to management.

Irrigation Projects

Three ODA evaluations were reviewed for this paper:

a 'Wadi Dhuleil, Jordan. An Ex-Post Evaluation'. E. Clayton, I. Carruthers, F. Hamawi. 1974

b 'Land Use and Socio-Economic Changes Under the Impact of Irrigation in the Lam Pao Project Area in Thailand'. School of Oriental and African Studies team. March 1978

c 'The North Sumatra Sprinkler Project of 1971: An Ex-Post Evaluation.' G. Allanson, September 1979.

These three projects have yielded positive results which have demonstrated that the beneficiaries have enjoyed higher incomes, despite the management problems experienced at the Wadi Dhuleil project in Jordan. All three projects involved surface irrigation but the Sumatra project included a relatively sophisticated sprinkler irrigation system and was not directly applicable to small-scale growers.

These three evaluation studies are scarcely sufficient for any ODA policy implications to result. Thus, ODA has had to base much of its policy adjustments on its vast wealth of experience and the work carried out on its behalf by other organisations such as studies by Wye College and the Institute of Development Studies (IDS), the irrigation management network of the Overseas Development Institute (ODI) and evaluation studies by other donor agencies.

A recent IBRD Working Paper: 'Economic Returns to Investment in Irrigation in India', IBRD Working Paper No. 536, brought to the fore some relevant points for future policies. With reference to surface irrigation systems it points out that:

a Management is a key issue especially with regard to water distribution

b Investment in irrigation had been economically appropriate and advantageous

c Rates of return to public projects have been low, but acceptable.

For groundwater schemes it found that:

a Technical design was most important

b A more reliable electricity supply was needed, along with credit and agricultural extension

c Due to the small size of agricultural plots, land consolidation is necessary to achieve more technically efficient size

d Public projects experienced managerial and technical problems and their effect was limited.

These results and those from other sources have directed ODA to aim its policies at improved management, taking into account the socio-economic conditions of water users and the need to develop effective and equitable arrangements to distribute water within the command area. There is an increasing worldwide perception of the technical, managerial, political and social factors that limit the utilisation of expensive and scarce water resources.

In Asia, the greater part of ODA effort has been directly or indirectly in groundwater exploitation. In Africa, the potential for irrigation is limited by high cost as well as the management difficulties outlined above. There is nevertheless scope for small-scale irrigation from groundwater or valley bottom schemes. Such small-scale, self-help schemes are becoming more important where the local community has demonstrated its ability and motivation to embark on projects of its own, assisted by outside finance and management. Such successes have been demonstrated by the small-scale irrigation scheme in Swaziland financed previously by ODA and managed by ODA Overseas Service Aid Scheme (OSAS)* officers. The Commonwealth Development Corporation (CDC) has also shown how small-scale growers can raise their income through the combination of irrigation and the cultivation of high-value crops, eg Mwea in Kenya.

Farm Power Projects

The results of the three farm power projects evaluated by ODA's Evaluation Department demonstrate relative success. These are:

a 'British Aid Tractors in India'. G. E. Dalton. 1976

b 'Tractor Hire Pools, Swaziland Experience'. A. A. Metianu, S. J. Pollard, A. Simons. 1979

c 'Oxenisation in The Gambia'. H. M. Mettrick. 1978.

The first of the three projects was the introduction of British tractors to India with credit provided for purchase. The evaluation set out to assess the social costs and benefits of the machines, including their effects on employment and food production. It was found that production did increase but more due to larger areas having been cultivated and that they were not employment-displacing. This conclusion is in contradiction with most accepted ideas that tractorisation is generally employment-displacing as widely expounded by H. P. Bingswanger† in his paper on the economics of tractor use in South Asia.† Dalton's evaluation showed that the negative employment effects were offset by increasing areas going into cultivation and the higher yields being generally achieved. He also showed that casual labour usage had increased.

The Swaziland Tractor Hire Pool evaluation also indicated positive results but it did point out that the hire charges were insufficient to meet the full costs of operation. This must be remedied but it may yet prove a difficult task for political reasons. The final farm power project evaluated was Oxenisation in The Gambia. This project has shown mixed success. The oxenisation

*The Overseas Service Aid Scheme (OSAS) meets part of the cost of qualified British staff employed by the governments of developing countries until local personnel can be trained to take over the work. ODA supplements the salaries paid by overseas governments and meets the cost of passages and other allowances.
†See bibliography on page 61.

programme has only affected primary cultivations, so limiting its impact but it is suggested that family income has increased by around 10–20 per cent. The social aspects are less positive since only the larger and richer farmers have benefited and there has been no benefit accruing to women who farm swamp rice.

In general, even though these latter evaluations have shown some success, ODA's policy has tended in recent years to adopt a more cautious approach to farm mechanisation programmes. This caution has been a result of the research by Bingswanger; studies by Morris and Pollard at the National Institute for Agricultural Engineering (NIAE); University of Reading report 'Farm Power in Bangladesh'; J. Farrington's work in Sri Lanka*; and feedback from many other sources. In particular, an article titled 'How Small Tractors Can Stall Development' in *International Agricultural Development,* November/December 1981, spells out very clearly some of the major problems:

a 80–90 per cent of ldc land-holdings are less than 5 ha; they are often fragmented, have complex tenurial patterns; these conditions are not conducive to the efficient use of tractors

b Mechanisation investment is lumpy and expensive

c Generally, yields and prices are low with little prospects of returns on investment unless a large hectarage can come under the plough; the crops cultivated are high value cash crops and a package of inputs is included in the cropping system

d Mechanisation can be labour-displacing yet can also cause labour bottlenecks at harvest if not carried through to the end of the process

e Mechanisation does not necessarily guarantee higher yields per unit of land

f Mechanisation uses up scarce foreign exchange.

Morris concludes that a multidisciplinary approach to mechanisation and a detailed assessment of needs and resources at farm level are required in order to set the physical and financial parameters needed for mechanisation to make its contribution to development.

In addition, the majority of tractor pools, despite the relative success of the Swaziland experience (which can be attributed to the relatively good infrastructure, and access to spares in neighbouring South Africa), have not been successful due to poor management, lack of funds and spare parts, heavy subsidies and poor crop returns.

ODA's caution concerning mechanisation has been seen to have developed due to the continuing inconclusiveness of current opinions. In its policy of helping the poor groups in rural societies, the search for more appropriate technology and a greater emphasis on building up knowledge of local farming systems has to some degree directed policy away from tractorisation and towards animal draught. Even so, there may still be a role for tractors in Africa where labour and not land is the major constraint and where scarce foreign exchange is not dissipated on fuel, eg Nigeria, which produces its own oil.

*See bibliography on page 61.

Commodity projects

Evaluation feedback on commodity projects has been mixed. Commodities projects have often been an integral part of other projects, eg irrigation or settler schemes. The 'Kenya Smallholder Tea Scheme' has been shown to be a success, mainly attributable to good management. The 'Coconut Development Project' in the Pacific Islands 'did not appear successful as there were insufficient returns to his (the farmer's) efforts' (cf J. C. H. Morris's paper). In general though, investment in beverage crops has not shown good returns due to the low price elasticity of demand in world markets. This marketing aspect is probably the most important factor which contributes to success or failure of a commodity project. For the small farmer who cannot absorb a high degree of risk, a stable market for his product is of prime importance, as well as a guarantee of a continuity in prices. In addition the commodity producer is defenceless against developed country tariffs as, for example, those imposed by the European Community (EC) against processed cotton. Most successful commodity projects have been those associated with processing units such as sugar- or fruit-growing where the grower has the protection of a large institution which absorbs some of the market risks and produces a higher value end product. This is brought out in respect of the Mumias Sugar Scheme in the ODI evaluation of ODM Aid to Kenya by G. Holtham and A. Hazlewood, which was published as a book *Aid and Inequality in Kenya*. However, it should be noted that this scheme has been criticised on account of various sociological problems inherent in the system of outgrowing adopted.

The marketing and economic environment must also be examined carefully when considering commodity programmes. It is pointless introducing or promoting crops where the producing nation cannot compete efficiently or in economies of scale against more powerful competitors or neighbours, eg South American countries v USA, where protectionism is rife, or where pricing policies are out of line due to overvalued exchange rates (eg Tanzania). These three aspects must be examined closely before introducing commodity projects.

Fisheries projects

ODA's fishing projects are very varied and geographically scattered. Up to the present there have been few evaluations and these have concentrated primarily on the technical side of projects. The most important fisheries project evaluation to date is 'Fisheries Development in Kiribati 1970–1980' by R. Lawson and W. Appleyard. The results were positive. Two further projects are under review: the Port Sudan and Seychelles projects.

Initial conclusions from the evaluation studies are that material aid such as boats, fishing gear and processing equipment will continue to be needed for the further development of traditional fisheries; that there will be increased effort on the utilisation of by-catches and in the fishing of unconventional fish species; that there will be more projects involving fish culture and research into means of reducing fish waste which accounts for 20 per cent of the global catch; and that British expertise (technical co-operation officers) and OSAS will continue to play a critical role in these developments.

Forestry projects

Two major forestry projects have been evaluated by ODA: the 'Imatong Mountains Forestry Project, Southern Sudan' and 'Forest Development in the Solomon Islands 1965–1980'. The main lessons drawn from these two evaluations (supplemented by wider experience generally) may be summarised as follows:

a *Monitoring.* The importance of technical monitoring by professional advisers as 'an integral part of project implementation' is clearly demonstrated in both projects. For example in the Solomons project the technical problems highlighted in the evaluation report (aspects of plant production, weed control, professional supervision, transport etc) had all been identified earlier in reports by the Forestry Adviser, action had been advised, and improvements had been initiated, to solve the major problems during the life of the project. The monitoring reports were therefore of direct benefit in the field as well as to the subsequent evaluation exercise

b *Scale.* Although not high in cost *forestry* projects are unusually extensive in both time and space. They commonly cover only the initial or an interim stage in a continuing process within which any evaluation must try to predict an outcome at some future date, perhaps 10 or 15 years later, on the evidence of what has been achieved so far. In a forest regeneration project, for example, the survival rates, growth rates and various aspects of quality (and therefore value) of the trees and the timber, change during the life of the crop in ways and at speeds which are not exactly predictable. The surrounding conditions (eg climate, vegetation, and other biotic factors) and market opportunities also change and affect final economic performance. Combined with the very extensive nature of forestry projects, covering often difficult and inaccessible terrain, this need for constant revision of project performance, involving a range of professional judgements, illustrates further the essential rôle of monitoring *vis à vis* periodic evaluation

c *Social benefit.* The relative remoteness or isolation of forestry projects can yield positive benefits in rural development, as evidenced by both the projects examined. As governments become more aware of the direct importance of forestry for social and community benefit ODA projects aimed directly at these objectives are likely to increase in number and scale, as implied in the paper, and this is now starting to happen

d *'Faulty project design'.* The imputation of faulty design as a general characteristic of forestry projects would be misleading. With hindsight it would be remarkable if all aspects of the project were found to be faultless, and the important lesson from both projects examined is that they were judged *successful* despite great and unforeseen difficulties. However delays in procurement of equipment are certainly a common and continuing feature of many projects and one which should be emphasised with a view to improving ODA procurement procedures. A general lesson to be drawn is that in the generalising act of evaluation (and then the evaluation of evaluations, as here) there is a danger of losing sight of the importance of choosing forestry projects which are in general sufficiently robust and central to aid objectives to succeed despite the inevitable uncertainties in their execution.

Livestock projects

Conclusions from livestock evaluations have been difficult to draw due to the long-term time scale that characterises them, as for example, with genetic improvement programmes or pasture upgrading schemes. As a result many evaluations have tended to yield rather negative results. These are exemplified by A. J. Cronin's 'Kenya Second Livestock Development Project', which concludes that the project in question was not achieving its objectives. This conclusion also agrees with the comments by Walter Goldschmidt in 1980:

> 'The picture that emerges from this review is one of almost unrelieved failure. Nothing seems to work, few pastoral people's lives have improved; there is no evidence of increased production of milk and meat; the land continues to deteriorate and millions of dollars have been spent.'

In addition to ODA's evaluation study, Stephen Sandford of ODI completed a comprehensive study of livestock activities in dry tropical Africa in January 1981 for the IBRD. He concluded, from this study of 34 projects, that:

a Rates of return were low; disbursements slow and completion dates delayed

b Ranching projects were too large, too complex and too reliant on expatriates

c Veterinary projects offered the highest social welfare alternative

d In project design, more attention to employment-creating aspects, research and training was needed

e An integrated approach covering sector policy, tenure problems and marketing was necessary

f A full understanding of the system was needed before the commencement of project implementation.

In contrast to these gloomy evaluations has been the work done by the livestock section of the 'British Tropical Agricultural Mission (BTAM)' in Bolivia, evaluated by J. Crossley and C. E. Johnson in 1977 and Dr M. Simpson's 'Evaluation of the Colombian Sheep Project' which is due to be submitted in the near future. Both of these studies have shown relative success with the BTAM evaluation quoting a 20 per cent increase in the average carcass weight of animals slaughtered at the abattoirs which, in part, was attributable to the work of the British Mission. The Columbian sheep project, even though it cited many faults in the original project emphasis and implementation, was also able to point out that the project built up considerable knowledge of sheep and cattle diseases in the area. In general though, veterinary projects have proved more successful and have yielded significant results. Examples are the Lesotho and Malawi projects for the control of foot-and-mouth- and tick-transmitted diseases. These latter projects have lowered national levels of the above diseases and resulted in benefit–cost ratios above unity. In addition the Development Assistance Committee (DAC) of the Organisation for Economic Cooperation and

The scene in the Lecture Hall, with Mr R. A. Browning at the rostrum.

Dr R. E. Cracknell, Head of ODA Evaluation Unit (now Evaluation Department), explains the organisation and work of his Unit

Development (OECD) has concluded that the size of the financial resources allotted to the livestock sector does not adequately reflect the significance of animal production in relation to GNP and exports. The DAC recommends that:

a More attention should be given to the livestock sector by donor agencies in order to increase the amount of external aid to these operations

b External aid should concentrate on sectoral animal production program-mes instead of on specific development projects which are not adequate to the complexity of, and the inter-actions within, the livestock sector; and

c Programmes should clearly identify target groups and make sure that the operation benefits actually reach these groups through appropriate market-ing and pricing policies.

Many of these recommendations have been accepted by ODA and have become the foundation of future policy direction. It is agreed that veterinary projects offer the best chances of success and can benefit all levels of society, reaching even the poorest. Their very success can however lead to problems in that the bottleneck effect of other constraints can become ever more severe, for example nutrition management and livestock marketing. Improvements in these areas should parallel the veterinary projects. As to projects attempting to increase production directly by improved nutrition, more emphasis must be put on understanding the farm systems and marketing.

Livestock projects in Asia should take account of the role of draught animals in the farm power/soil fertility complex, with research focusing on byproducts as an animal nutrition source.

Final Remarks and Conclusions

Despite the limited number of evaluations reviewed in this paper, some important implications are:

a Preliminary research into the farming systems is necessary before project implementation to produce policies that are appropriate technically, economically and socially

b Realistic assessment must be made of the likely benefits and time scale. Previous projects, especially IRDPs, have had high rates of return calculated during the appraisal stage that have often proved totally unrealistic

c In project implementation, markets, price policies and the existing institutions must be taken into account. A project cannot be successful unless sectoral policies and institutions are appropriate

d Where the economic situation is considered inhospitable to agricultural development, the question of which type of aid is more appropriate must be posed. Is project aid necessarily the best choice? Sector or programme aid may provide a better option

e With regard to multisectoral projects, the correct balance must be struck between productive activities and 'social services'.

The bibliography for this section follows the discussion.

Discussion

Mr F. G. Holder (Director, Evaluation Service, United Nations/Food and Agriculture Organisation (UN/FAO) World Food Programme (WFP)) congratulated the authors on putting together such a concise and accurate summary of the problems affecting rural development projects. His organisation had experienced very similar problems.

He suggested that a basic deficiency on the part of the planners was their failure to adequately consult local people. It was not always necessary to set up a sophisticated feasibility study or sample survey. If one got together a group of say 50 local people for a couple of hours, one could get a very clear picture of what was being grown and why, what their needs were and the changes they were seeking. His department had done this recently and the results had completely turned on their head the views that had been expressed by the decision-makers in the capital city. It was important to go right down to the farm level and to ask the intended beneficiaries what they really wanted.

As to markets and pricing policies these were basic issues that needed specialist attention. A market economist was needed to advise the government on how to achieve that delicate balance between the price required to give the producer an adequate incentive on the one hand, and the price that would be fair to the consumer and which would not price the country out of export markets on the other. Usually such advice was only sought and given after it had become apparent that the crops were not forthcoming, and by then it was often too late.

Dr M. Lipton (Institute of Development Studies (IDS), University of Sussex) asked if any of the ODA's evaluations had thrown light on the World Bank's rural sociologists' recent finding that where in-depth research on likely rates of adoption of new techniques have been carried out before the project started the realised rate of return was close to, or even better than, the expected rate of return; whereas in those cases where no research had been carried out beforehand the results were usually worse than expected. He quoted a long-term research study in Sri Lanka carried out by J. Farrington of Farm Power which concluded that the large-scale spread of tractors in Sri Lanka had proved very disappointing in its impact because insufficient attention had been paid to the innovations and improvements in water management that were necessary when switching from water buffaloes to tractors.

Dr Lipton asked if the ODA evaluations looked at the distribution of benefits between rich and poor people and whether a comparison was made with a control group.

Dr Lipton's third point related to the difference between Asia and Africa. He felt that rather than comparing economic and social factors it was more useful to compare the ecologies in different regions. Some ecological situations in Africa were similar to those in Asia (eg the semi-arid area of North-East Botswana was comparable to parts of Western India) and it would be worthwhile comparing technological developments in the two places. Why for instance was it that in Africa minor irrigation systems (low-life pumps or tubewells) which would be automatically used for intensive cropping in Asia were used for cattle watering which seems to be a rather wasteful use of resources? Perhaps evaluations could throw some light on these issues. Then again, why was it that millett and sorghum yields were so much lower in Africa than in Asia, even for very similar ecologies, and why was it that simple locally produced technologies such as seed drills, appropriate ploughs and so on, which were taken for granted in Asia, were generally not available in many parts of Africa? In short there seemed to be an agricultural technology gap which it might be useful for evaluations to investigate.

Mr A. R. Ayazi (Chief, Evaluation Service, FAO, Rome) also stressed the need for evaluations to identify the beneficiaries. In parts of Asia a farmer with half an acre of land might be considered rich, but that would not be so in Africa. Much more time needed to be spent during the preparation stage of projects in identifying the likely beneficiaries.

Relevant to this issue was the question of who benefited from expenditure on agricultural research. Studies had demonstrated that agricultural research could yield high overall rates of return but this begged the question of whether the benefits went mainly to the rich farmers or to the poor. The high-yielding varieties seemed to have benefited mainly the rich farmers and so far relatively little attention had been given to the needs of the dryland farmers in upland areas. Moreover the small farmer had different needs from the large farmer. He might not be willing or able to adopt a high-input/high-output technology: he had to give priority to food security and basic subsistence needs, and as he seldom hired labour he had to give priority to the family labour situation. He was necessarily very concerned about stability of income and the need to minimise risk.

Another relevant issue was that of the diffusion of improved technologies for the welfare of the farmer. The problems were area-specific and culture-specific and the sociologist or anthropologist probably had as much to contribute as the economist or the technologist. More interchange of experience was needed between developing countries: there were countries where great improvements had been introduced in millett or sorghum production whereas only 100 kilometres away, say on the other side of the border, no one seemed to be aware of it. This was a problem that the Consultative Group on International Agricultural Research (CGIAR) might well tackle.

Professor D. Colman (University of Manchester) agreed with the need to identify beneficiaries, especially the extent to which benefits were going to the smaller farmers, but he pointed out that small farmers were not a homogenous group—rather they were a series of sub-groups: in fact there was a complex set of interacting sub-groups, with some farmers apparently incapable of responding whilst others were very active and responsive to stimuli. Until a model was available of these complex interactions it was difficult to see how the mere targeting of benefits to help the poorest, in itself would be successful. He suggested that baseline studies should be used to develop such a model.

Mr A. A. Kingshotte (Evaluation Department, ODA) suggested that one reason why so many rural development projects failed was that the local people had not been sufficiently involved in the planning and management of develop-ment schemes—there had been too much 'top-down' planning and dictation from the capital city.

He queried whether farmers were in fact slow to adopt innovations. His own experience (and this had been supported by the evaluations) had shown that in Africa, particularly where an innovation was clearly profitable to the farmer in the broad sense (ie in terms of all the factors such as markets, prices, transport, labour, labour availability and so on), farmers had been quick to adopt it. Over-optimistic assumptions of adoption rates were usually due to the innovations being less than fully appropriate. For example, all too often people had been pushing a high-cost innovation for a low-value crop.

Mr R. D. Bell (National Institute of Agricultural Engineering (NIAE)) felt that too little attention had been paid to the role of the middlemen. They had an important task to perform and if organisational systems were introduced aimed at cutting out the middleman this could often lead to serious problems. Dr Gwyer had mentioned the Sind Land Levelling Project and Mr Bell suggested that one of the main reasons for its success was that a wide spectrum of the community had benefited including the landowners and the suppliers of equipment whilst the government officials were pleased with the organisational aspects. There had been a big increase in employment and there were benefits for sharecroppers which had pleased the poorer people. For a project to succeed it usually had to satisfy people over a wide income spectrum.

Referring to Dr Lipton's comments on the lack of success with the Sri Lanka Tractor Project, Mr Bell said that the crucial factor was the price of water. If this were very low people would not go out of their way to conserve it. The Sri Lankan Project would be unlikely to succeed until there was a reasonable water pricing policy based on consumption.

Mr P. J. Wood (Department of Forestry, University of Oxford) suggested that forestry (by which he meant the process of growing the trees) might present something of a special case. Firstly there was the long time cycle, ie if one were planning for 15 years ahead it might be almost impossible to identify the likely beneficiaries so far in the future. Secondly there was the difficulty of estimating yields over such a long period when there could well be important gains from improved management, genetic improvements, etc. This re-inforced Dr Gwyer's comments on the need for effective monitoring as a feed-in to the eventual evaluation. If there had been no monitoring in the meantime it would be very difficult to evaluate a project 15 or 20 years after its commencement. The yield aspect in particular called for careful monitoring because appraisers had a tendency to use conservative estimates and in several cases that he knew of the actual yields had turned out to be double what had been expected. Without careful monitoring one might find oneself with twice as much timber to fell and market as had been expected. Finally there was the question of price movements over such a long period of years—these could well turn a project on its head.

Dr I. Carruthers (Wye College) commented that Dr Gwyer had asked for more formal and more consistent presentation of evaluation reports, but he felt this might be difficult to achieve because it was still too early and evaluation techniques were still rapidly changing. There seemed to be a conflict between the attempt of many evaluators on the one hand to look over their shoulders at the precepts of the academic world and on the other to produce realistic and pragmatic reports (often more down to earth than the various manuals that aid agencies and academics had been producing). There was a problem in this because it was intimidating local professionals who were afraid they were not doing good solid professional work simply because they could not reach the standards set by the so-called 'practical' manuals. He had recently spent some time in Indonesia and he was disturbed by the cynical manipulation of the appraisal and evaluation processes by professionals that he had seen there. It had got to such a state that the whole of economic analysis was likely to be discredited. The problems had been accentuated in recent years because in addition to the economists there were now agriculturalists forecasting yields and doing discounting and engineers producing internal rates of return, since these were now required to get the job done. ODA should be aware of the manipulation, forced assumptions and massaging of data that was going on and should consider how it was going to handle the situation if credibility were to be maintained.

Dr R. M. Lawson (Consultant Fisheries Economist, Centre for Fisheries Studies, Humberside College of Higher Education) responding to the Chairman's invitation to talk about her experience in evaluating ODA fishery projects, first gave some background to the fisheries of Kiribati which she had examined and then summarised the main lessons. First the evaluation had shown that the colonial government and local administrators had wasted a lot of time in the early days because they thought they could go it alone without taking advice from ODA's Principal Fisheries Adviser: after 14 years it had been proved that he had been right all along. Secondly one clear lesson was that developing countries should not dabble in fisheries without taking professional advice, and that applied especially to joint venture agreements. The Japanese were highly skilled negotiators and small developing countries needed expert help. Fishing development required a lot of research on basic resources, on types of gear and on the needs of the fishermen. No donor should make aid funds available unless these aspects had been adequately researched.

As to the ODA's own procedures, Dr Lawson was critical of the ODA filing system. She had been given files stacked three feet high and it had taken a long time for her to sort out the key documents from among the mass of routine letters and minutiae. It would have helped if the key documents had been placed on a separate project file.

Finally, Dr Lawson referred to the need to carry out baseline studies covering such aspects as employment, rural–urban drift, what was happening to the extended family, the changing role of women and the impact of spreading education in causing people to leave primary production. These aspects all needed careful monitoring, as did demographic change. Taken as a whole the story of fisheries development in Kiribati had been one of success, albeit rather slow, but perhaps with natural resources development aid projects this was the surest way to success.

Responding to the discussion, *Dr G. D. Gwyer (Economist, ODA)* agreed with Mr Ayazi about the need for more consultation with local people. ODA had endorsed the proposals for rapid rural appraisal that had emanated from the Institute of Development Studies (IDS), ie as a complement to more rigorous forms of analysis rather than as an alternative.

Dr Lipton had asked if ODA's evaluations had thrown light on the importance of prior research into attitudes to the adoption of new techniques. So far as he knew the ODA's evaluations did not focus on this aspect, except possibly the work on the Kosi Hills Area Rural Development Programme (KHARDEP) Project in Eastern Nepal. Dr Lipton had also asked if ODA used control groups and the KHARDEP Project was one such example. There an attempt had been made to look at the nutritional status of particular groups within the project and for a control group outside it. Similar techniques had been used in India in association with the Council of Applied Economic Research.

Dr Lipton had raised the question of comparisons between Africa and Asia but Dr Gwyer doubted whether much could be gained from such a comparison. For example the World Bank had evaluated a very successful smallholder rubber development project in North Sumatra and had tried to transfer the design to a country in West Africa where the population density was much lower and it had failed; it should have taken into account such factors as labour and land ratios. The reason why he had emphasised Asia and Africa was that at one point he thought that higher management in ODA was tending to extrapolate African experience on some kinds of projects to Asia. Also he had observed that in West Africa attempts were being made to introduce technologies developed at the International Rice Research Institute (IRRI) in the Philippines whereas the socio-ecology in Africa was not appropriate.

Mr Ayazi had stressed the difficulty of identifying the beneficiaries and he agreed. He said that ODA fully recognised the difficulty of getting official aid to rural societies but still thought the attempt was worth making. As to the question of research benefits to dryland farmers, he thought that some of the international centres notably the International Crop Research Institute for the Semi-Arid Tropics (ICRISAT), the International Centre for Agricultural Research in Dry Areas (ICARDA) and possibly the International Institute for Tropical Agriculture (IITA), were concerned with the problems of dryland farming. The basic philosophy of ICRISAT was that the seed itself should be sufficient as far as possible, ie extensive use of fertilisers, which involved an element of risk, should not be absolutely necessary.

Dr Colman had raised the question of the heterogeneity of small farmers. However in some countries, such as India, there were fairly clearly recognisable groups of people who could be labelled as 'marginal', 'small' or 'landless'. Admittedly people might sometimes pretend to be in one category or another, to benefit from subsidies, but there was no doubt that the categories existed. Dr Gwyer mentioned the work of P. Hazell and his colleagues in the International Food Policy Research Institute (IFPRI) into the nature of rural–urban intersectoral linkages. The implications of this work were that the best way to help the poorest people in society might be not to aim at the poorest in rural areas but at the middle-income earners. His work was based on the Muda River Irrigation Project study in Northwestern Malaysia*.

*See bibliography on page 63.

It was still only a theory and the study had not yet been completed.

Dr Carruthers had questioned the rather academic nature of ODA's Appraisal Manual but Dr Gwyer suggested that the ODA's Sector Manuals were more practical in their orientation. He agreed that the point about the cynical manipulation of data by economists and others was an important one and the economists should ask themselves whether they were tending to bend the rules to fulfil certain objectives which were not necessarily developmental.

References

Integrated Rural Development Projects

Devitt, P. 1978 'The Role of Sociological Factors in four ODM projects'

Imbert-Terry, A. 1980 'South Darfur Rural Development Project, Sudan. 1970–1980'

Morris, J. C. H. 1981 A Synopsis of Reviews of Six African Rural Development Projects:

  i ODA/IBRD joint supervision mission of the Upper Region Agricultural Development Project, Ghana (URADEP). September 1980. Report by J. C. H. Morris.

  ii Evaluation of South Darfur Rural Development Project (SRDP), Sudan. September 1980. Report by A. Imbert-Terry.

  iii Land Use Component, Tabora Rural Integrated Development Project (TRIDEP). Project Review. March 1981. ODA report by Stone/Robertson/Morris.

  iv A Review of the Basic Agricultural Services Project, Lesotho (BASP). March 1981. Report by Weare/Spens/Morris.

  v A Note on the Rural Development Areas Programme, Swaziland (RDAP). April 1981. Report by Weare/Spens/Morris.

  vi A Note on National Rural Development Programme, Malawi (NRDP). April 1981. Report by Weare/Spens/Morris.

Irrigation Projects

Agrarian Development Unit, Wye College, 1974 'Wadi Dhuleil, Jordan. An Ex-Post Evaluation'

Allanson, G. 1979 'The North Sumatra Sprinkler Project of 1971: An Ex-Post Evaluation'

School of Oriental and African Studies Team, 1978 'Land-Use and Socio-Economic Changes Under the Impact of Irrigation in the Lam Pao Project Area in Thailand'.

Farm Power Projects

Bingswanger, H. P. 1978 'The Economics of Tractors in South Asia'. Agricultural Development Council, NY, and ICRISAT, India

Dalton, G. E. 1976 'British Aid Tractors in India. An Ex-Post Evaluation'

Farrington, J. 1983 'Small Farm Capital in Sri Lanka. The Case of Draught Power'

Farrington, J. and Abeyratne, F. 1982 'Farm Power in Sri Lanka'. University of Reading, Department of Agricultural Economics and Management

Development Studies, 22 & 25
Metianu, A. A., Pollard, S. J., Simons, A. J. 1979 'Tractor Hire Pools:
Swaziland Experience'
Mettrick, H. 1978 'Oxenisation in The Gambia'.

Fisheries Projects

Gubbins, K. E., Maniece, A. 1978 'Aid to Fisheries 1970–1976'
Lawson, R. M., Appleyard, W. P. 1982 'An Evaluation of ODA Assistance to
Fisheries Development in Kiribati. 1970–1980'.

Forestry Projects

Gane, M., Plumptre, R. A., Ellis, C. I. 1982 'Evaluation Study of Imatong
Mountains Forestry Project, Southern Sudan'
Wood, P. J., Watt, G. R. 1982 'An Evaluation of British Aid to Assist Forest
Development in the Solomon Islands. 1965–1980'.

Commodity Programmes

Ackroyd, P. J. 1976 'Coconut Development'
Hall, J. M. 1971 'The Chikwawa Cotton Development Project'
Hebblethwaite, M. J. 1979 'An Economic Analysis of the Social Returns to
Phase II of the Malawi Smallholder Tea Scheme'
Stern, N. H. 1970 'An Appraisal of Smallholder Tea in Kenya'.

Livestock

Cronin, A. J. 1978 'Kenya Second Livestock Development Project'
Putt, S. N. H., Shaw, A. P. M. 'An Evaluation of the Control of Sheep Scab in
Lesotho and the Control of Foot-and-Mouth- and Tick-Transmitted
Diseases in Malawi'
Simpson, M. 1983 'Evaluation of the Colombian Sheep Project'.

Technical Co-operation/Institutes

Crossley, J., Johnson, C. 1977 'Work of the British Tropical Agricultural
Mission in Bolivia'.

Related References

Couteras, A., Gregersen, H. 'Policy Considerations in Forestry Project
Evaluations'. *Journal of Forestry*, June 1982
FAO. CERES. 'FAO Review on Agriculture and Development'
Gill, G. J. 1981 'Farm Power in Bangladesh, Volume I.' University of
Reading, Department of Agricultural Economics and Management.
Development Study No. 19
IBRD, 1982 Fishery Sector Policy Paper
James, P. 1981 'Farm Power in Bangladesh'. War on Want Occasional Paper
No. 1
Lawson, R. M. 'Post-evaluation of fisheries projects in Marine Policy' *The
International Journal for Economics, Planning and Politics of Ocean Exploitation*
Volume 4, No. 1, January 1980
Mettrick, H. M., James, D. P. 1981 'Farm Power in Bangladesh', Volume 2.
University of Reading, Department of Agricultural Economics and
Management

Morris, J., Pollard, S. 'How Small Tractors can Stall Development', in *International Agricultural Development*, November/December 1981
NIAE. Report on a visit to Sierra Leone, June 1982
ODA Sector Appraisal Manual: Miscellaneous Investment Proposals. August 1980
ODA Economic Paper No (81)1. Agricultural Development and Aid Policy, June 1981
ODA 1982 UK Experience with Identifying and Implementing Poverty-Related Aid Projects
OECD DAC Evaluation of Projects and Operations, October 1982
Seig, M. 'The Cotton Business', in *Development and Co-operation* No. 1/1981. (January/February).

Other Evaluation Studies of Natural Resources Topics

Ansell, A., Upton, M. University of Reading, Department of Agricultural Economics and Management, 1979 'Small Scale Water Storage and Irrigation'
Clayton, E. 1978 'A Comparative Study of Settlement Schemes in Kenya'
Crapper, D. G., Harrison, J., Waddell, R. L. 1980 'Toledo Rural Development Project, Belize. A Review'
Dickie, A. University of Reading, Department of Agricultural Economics and Management, 1981 'Group Farming in North West Nigeria'
Dening, R. C. 1980 FAO/UK/HFCL. 'Dryland Farming Fertiliser Educational Project, Indore, Madhya Pradesh, India'
ODA Report. 1980 'UK/Indonesia Groundwater Monitoring Visit'
Peers, A. W., Gwyer, G. D. 1982 'Indo-British Fertiliser Education Project'. ODA Report on Monitoring Visit
Shaxson, T. F., Sweetman, J., Long, P. B. R., Hudson, N. W. 1979 'The Indo–UK Dryland Farming Operational Research Project'. Vols 1 and 2.

Other Related Studies

Bottrall, A. F. World Bank Staff Working Paper No. 334, 1976 'Comparative Study of the Management and Organisation of Irrigation Projects'
Grindle, R. Odupoy, R. 1977 'Economic Losses Resulting from Cystericecus Bovis Infestation in Kenya'
IBRD 1981. 'Indonesia Transmigration Program Review'
IBRD 1982. Project Evaluation in Regional Perspective: A Study of an Irrigation Project in Northwest Malaysia (C. Bell, P. Hazell, R. Slade)
McCauley, E., Stoops, D., Lindgren, H. 1973 'Survey of Successful Experience in Assisting the Smallholder Livestock Producer'
McInerney, J., Donaldson, G. World Bank Staff Working Paper No. 210, 1975 'The Consequences of Farm Tractors in Pakistan'
Rarkes, P., Amam, V. University of Makerere, Uganda 1974 'Project Appraisal and Evaluation in Agriculture'
Schuh, G., Tollirr, H. World Bank Staff Working Paper No. 360, 1979 'Costs and Benefits of Agricultural Research: the State of the Art'.

B2

Infrastructure
by Mrs J. M. White, Economist, Transport and Road Research Laboratory (TRRL), Department of the Environment

Introduction

ODA has carried out, or is in the process of carrying out, 12 ex-post evaluation studies in the roads sector, while four further road evaluation studies have been undertaken under the guidance of the Overseas Unit of the TRRL. The majority of these studies have examined road projects in Africa, nine out of a total of 16, while the other studies draw on projects from the Far East, the Pacific and Central America. In addition ODA has undertaken three ex-post evaluation studies of other transport projects, a bridge project, a deep-water harbour project and a package of assistance to the railway sector in one country. The scope of these studies has been wide-ranging. Some have had as their major objective to see what lessons can be learnt to improve ODA's project appraisal methodology, others to judge whether the assumptions on which the investment was originally justified have held up, while others have been concerned with how to improve efficiency at the implementation stage. This paper summarises ODA's main findings from its ex-post evaluation studies in the transport sector.

Roads: Lessons for Appraisal Methodology

For appraisal purposes roads can be divided into two broad categories:

a Those where baseline traffic flows are so low that the conventional vehicle operating cost savings approach is not valid and where the justification for road investment rests on its expected impact on rural and agricultural development

b Those where baseline traffic flows are sufficiently high to allow the appraisal to concentrate primarily on direct benefits to future traffic flows.

These are considered separately below.

Roads with Low Baseline Traffic Flows

Many case studies in different parts of the world have often pointed to significant development benefits stemming from rural road investment. These studies have largely been carried out in untypical isolated locations where the road investment has brought about large changes in transport costs often arising from a change in transport mode from, for example, headloading to vehicle transport. More usually rural road planning is concerned with less dramatic projects to improve existing roads and tracks, where no change in transport mode is envisaged. ODA's experience in this more typical road investment planning environment has been that rural roads have had little impact on rural and agricultural development.

There have been two comprehensive evaluation studies in Africa, one in Sierra Leone[4]* and the other in Ghana[16], which have looked at the role of feeder roads in promoting rural and agricultural change. In Sierra Leone a sampling frame of 412 farming households was chosen within which one group of households was within an area benefiting from an integrated agricultural development project and the other outside the area. These two groups of households were then further sub-divided into those who were close to feeder roads and those who were further away from the roads. Analysis of some two hundred variables showed basic homogeneity in the study area between the four categories of households. Agricultural activity was very similar throughout the area while most households participated significantly in the cash economy. The main identifiable benefit of the feeder road programme was that the extension service appeared to be concentrating its efforts on accessible (ie roadside) communities, while roadside farmers were slightly more likely to have a higher proportion of their land under tree cash crops, and to be making greater use of fertilisers than their non-roadside counterparts. These differences were small however.

In Ghana a cross-sectional study of 491 households in 33 villages was carried out in order to determine how agricultural practices, costs and prices varied with accessibility within the Ashanti region. Little evidence was found to suggest that agriculture was adversely affected by inaccessibility, apart from some difficulty in obtaining loan finance by farmers in the more remote areas. Also the more accessible villages were observed to have a higher proportion of people employed outside agriculture. The reason advanced for the study's conclusions was that the improvement of existing road surfaces had a negligible effect on the prices received by the farmer for agricultural produce (farmgate prices). Transport cost savings per unit of produce were extremely low. However, connecting a village to a roadhead by converting a footpath to a vehicle track was calculated to have a gross beneficial effect in the order of 100 times greater than improving the same distance of earth track (a motorable track) to good gravel road. This, of course, is an example of a situation where the transport mode changes, in this case from head-loading to vehicle transport.

A third study of the impact of a feeder road programme on agricultural change in Swaziland[1] concluded that economic activity had risen in some areas served by the roads, but not in others. No reasons for this difference were adduced. The approach taken by this ex-post evaluation study contrasts strongly with that taken by the two former studies. It was a short-term study which was greatly hampered by lack of data and which consequently was unable to provide any depth of analysis. It is a lesson in how not to go about an ex-post evaluation study of feeder roads, while the former two are models of how best to approach them. A successful evaluation, defined as relating cause and effect, depends, *inter alia*, on a long-term approach, during which time the evaluator generates his own specific data. Such data are not produced by the project itself. This approach is currently being adopted in two on-going road evaluation studies, one in Kenya[11], the other in Tanzania[5], where baseline data are being collected and progress monitored of certain key

---

*All references in this Section refer to the bibliography at the end.

aspects of the project over a lengthy period.

A number of the evaluations have clearly shown the importance of personal travel in total rural traffic flows. This is true of roads with both high and low baseline traffic flows. In the Kenyan example mentioned above between 65 to 80 per cent of all traffic moving (measured at three census points) comprised fare-paying passengers. Agricultural traffic was between five to ten per cent of traffic moving while the balance was government vehicles and private cars plus retail goods. In the earlier rural road appraisals very little attention was paid to passenger traffic and justification for rural road investment was sought from forecasted agricultural development and generated agricultural freight traffic. A good example of this approach is given by the Malawi study[2], where the expansion of the feeder road network was justified in terms of the expected outflow of agriculture produce over the life of the project. This analytical approach was widespread and although it is now known that passenger traffic is much more responsive to new road investment than freight traffic, there has been little statistical research undertaken to easily permit a reliable forecast of induced passenger traffic to be made. The present Kenyan road evaluation study is specifically looking at this aspect and it is hoped to be able to add to current knowledge on the elasticity of demand for personal travel in rural areas.

Roads with High Baseline Traffic Flows

Roads with higher baseline traffic volumes have proved less problematical both to appraise and to evaluate. This is because the direct benefits to traffic are the prime concern at both stages of analysis: it is a relatively easy matter to rank projects initially and to assess subsequently whether forecast benefits were realised. Two ex-post evaluation studies[9,10] did, in fact, re-work the economic rate of return shortly after construction was completed and both concluded that the project was still earning a good rate of return.

It has been generally recognised for some time that the higher-income groups in any country will benefit more than the lower-income groups from a road investment. A study of a new major inter-urban highway project in West Malaysia[18] specifically considered the question of who had benefited from the investment. Road users along a particular route were divided into seven broad income categories, both before and after the new highway opened. It was found that those in the higher income groups, those earning cash incomes above a given monthly sum, who comprised seven per cent of the employed population, gained 72 per cent of the total road user benefits arising from the opening of the new highway. Those in the lowest income group, who comprised 55 per cent of the employed population received less than one per cent of the benefits from the new highway. The Kenya study is also attempting to do a similar exercise for rural passenger traffic.

Only one evaluation study considered the value of time savings to passengers and to freight operators. This was the West Malaysia study[18,19] which found that journey-time savings were the major single benefit to passengers and car drivers from the new highway. The result for freight operations was more complex. It was found, using modal choice analysis, ie travellers can choose between faster but more expensive methods of travelling and slower but cheaper modes, that the value of time savings for road users was similar to that found by many studies for road users in developed countries. In both cases the value of time savings is expressed as a percentage of the average wage rate. This similarity probably reflects the fact that road users on major highways in West Malaysia come overwhelmingly from the modern sector of the economy and very few from the subsistence sector. The implications of this result for project appraisal methodology are firstly that benefits from major road projects are currently being underestimated in many cases, (where the value of time savings is not being included in the list of benefits) and secondly that further studies are needed to expand knowledge in this field.

Roads: Lessons for the Implementation of Projects

A very interesting engineering study on a major highway in Kenya[8] was carried out by the TRRL nine years after the road had been upgraded from an earth track to hardtop. It concluded that the road was in good condition at the time of the study although it had carried more than twice the weight of heavy traffic than the pavement design had envisaged at that date. It identified the most important reason for this successful outcome as being the good control exercised over the quality of construction, so that standards laid down were adhered to. The presence of very strong subgrades and good subbase material along the alignment plus adequate maintenance were also contributory features. It is not always the case that roads are built to specified standards, with the result that pavement failure occurs earlier than it would otherwise do. The conclusions of this study therefore have very important implications for road project implementation.

A second engineering study, which is still ongoing, is monitoring the progress of an experimental method of implementing a major highway project in Tanzania. In place of the normal form of contract, where contractors tender on the basis of priced bills of quantities plus contingencies, a price at which it was thought to be possible to carry out the construction was agreed between a contractor and the client. This has been named a target cost contract and was a response to the uncertainties surrounding a large construction project under difficult circumstances, and the unlikelihood of attracting any international engineering contractor to tender under normal tendering arrangements. Throughout the construction phase the client and the contractor jointly take decisions on issues and at the end of the day, any cost savings are divided equally between them. It is hoped that by this method the project will be completed either at a lower cost or at an earlier date than it would have been under the normal form of contract.

Feedback

ODA is currently drafting a new roads sector appraisal manual designed to help advisers in ODA who are called upon to prepare or give advice on specific projects in the roads sector. It is not intended to be a detailed guide to engineering practice and standards but will draw on the current state of knowledge in social, economic and technical fields in order to highlight areas of major concern to those planning projects in the roads sector. A number of issues that have been thrown up by ODA's ex-post evaluation studies of road projects will be useful case material for this exercise.

Other feedback from the evaluation studies will come in the form of suggested research topics to be undertaken by the Overseas Unit of TRRL. This Unit already carries out wide-ranging research on road transport issues in developing countries. Benefits from the research programme are maximised when the lessons learnt at the evaluation stage are fed back into research priorities.

Bridges

The Bosporus Bridge project in Turkey was subject to an ex-post evaluation by ODA five years after the bridge was opened to traffic at the end of 1973. The primary purpose of the bridge was to ease massive congestion problems caused by an overloaded ferry service. The need for a bridge was taken as given and the original appraisal adopted a cost–effectiveness and not a cost–benefit approach. By 1978 traffic flows over the bridge had exceeded the level forecast for 1990. Estimating future traffic flows is notoriously difficult, especially where a project involves major and not marginal changes in the transport network, as in this case. No advice is given here on how to improve traffic forecasting techniques, but rather on how to improve the presentation of traffic forecasts. This and other useful lessons for similar projects did emerge from the evaluation study.

Firstly, it is surprising, given the size and scale of the project (the bridge comprised a six-lane dual carriageway) that the implications for traffic flows in Istanbul itself were not considered, along with the need for possible technical co-operation (TC) assistance with traffic management policies. Secondly, the consultants glossed over the uncertainties in the traffic forecasts rather than emphasising them and stressing the need for flexibility in future toll policy, (and traffic management policies). Being presented with a single traffic forecast placed within the narrow analytical framework of traffic flows over the bridge, the Turkish authorities were ill-prepared to deal with the situation that emerged. A peaking problem rapidly arose, caused by commuters travelling to and from work in their own cars. The congestion could have been eased by a combination of measures, such as peak toll pricing, differential pricing discriminating against low-occupancy private cars, reversing lane flows during rush hours or by introducing bus lanes in Istanbul to encourage commuters to switch from cars to public transport. No corrective action was taken for four years, after which time tolls were raised. This partially solved the problem, but left the traffic management problem untouched. The lessons from the evaluation of the Bosporus Bridge project are therefore, (a) the larger the project the more important it is to consider the implications of alternative traffic growth rates, and (b) not to take too narrow a view of the ramifications of the project. These conclusions will be taken note of in the production of the bridges section of the new Roads Sector Manual.

Railways

In 1980 an evaluation was made of the outcome of four Projects and Evaluation Committee (PEC) submissions (1968, 1971, 1974 and 1979) proposing investments in Malawi Railways. An assessment was made of the main technical, economic and financial implications of the different projects.

The 1968 proposal covered the rehabilitation of the track north of Balaka. For a combination of reasons (including ODA's scepticism and insufficient interest by the Malawi Government) this project was not implemented. The 1971, 1974 and 1979 projects concentrated on the progressive rehabilitation of the track between Balaka and the southern border. By the end of 1980, this work had been largely implemented and was expected to be completed by 1982.

A major criticism to emerge from the evaluation was that there was a consistent failure to recognise the long-term ongoing need to review the whole of the track from Balaka to the southern border. This was in part attributed to the lack of railway expertise employed by ODA to carry out the original appraisals; ODA relied heavily on Malawi Railways for the technical input.

Because of the failure to consider the long-term nature of the problems faced by Malawi Railways mistakes were made in the economic justification of the projects. A 'hostage' type of appraisal was carried out whereby it was argued that without certain components of track rehabilitation then the line would have to close. Although it is correct to consider this position it is essential to identify *all* the future rehabilitation costs of the whole link length for a given planning time period. In order to make a proper assessment as to whether the line should remain open or not the total discounted costs of using the railway should be compared with the total discounted costs of using the next best alternative which in this case would be by road.

Unfortunately the three separate appraisals were partial in their analysis of the problem and hence at each stage there was an overstatement of the benefits of the investment and little guidance was given as to the future requirements for renewal that might be expected.

The evaluation also identified mistakes in estimating the benefits of rehabilitating lengths of track which in the absence of the rehabilitation would have required a drop in train speed. Wages, fuel, maintenance and capital costs were expressed in terms of costs per hour. The benefits from increased train speed were then calculated by multiplying these costs per train hour by the time saved. It was pointed out that this was likely to lead to gross overestimation of the benefits. It is very unlikely that wagons and train crews could be more fully used on the track length in question. Train maintenance costs are not functionally related to time in this way and fuel will more than likely be *saved* rather than lost by the train travelling more slowly.

Both the initial appraisals and the evaluation pointed to the poor financial performance of Malawi Railways, costs were tending to rise much faster than revenues. It appears that the Malawi government has been reluctant to allow tarriffs to increase by as much as the Railways would have liked possibly to help Malawi's exports and also to avoid triggering additional rises in tariffs on the railway through Mozambique on which Malawi is so dependent.

Feedback

As a result of this thorough ex-post evaluation study the ODA was able to prepare a Railways Manual drawing heavily on the lessons learnt from the study.

Ports

An ex-post evaluation of the Port Victoria scheme in the Seychelles was carried out two years after the port became fully operational. Before the construction of the new port goods had been handled to and from cargo ships by lighter, which was slow and expensive. The new deep-water port allowed ships to berth alongside and cargo to be handled directly from ship to shore. The evaluation study confirmed that the new port could be expected to show a healthy economic and financial rate of return, even though economic conditions in 1977 were less favourable to the Seychelles than those in 1971. However, the most interesting part of the study turned out to be an analysis of the distribution of the benefits of the new port.

The benefits of improved port efficiency are shared in the first instance between shipping companies and the countries they serve. Faster ship turnaround time is reflected in lower costs to the shipping companies. As no part of this was passed on to the Seychelles in the form of lower freight rates, since these were fixed on a regional and not an individual port basis, recommendations were made on appropriate increases in port charges. Cargo handling (stevedoring and shorehandling) was under the control of a private, foreign-owned company, rather than the more usual arrangement of being in the hands of a local company. Any benefits to this side of operations were therefore also going outside the Seychelles. An investigation of the terms of the cargo handling contract showed that they were unnecessarily generous. The company was being guaranteed a commercial rate of return for a risk-free operation for a ten-year period. Contracts for cargo handling are normally awarded on a one- or two-year basis on less favourable terms. Consequently, a significant proportion of the benefits of the new port were going to a foreign-owned company. It was recommended that the Seychelles government buy in a majority shareholding in the cargo handling company.

The Seychelles government has taken up a number of the recommendations made in the evaluation report, so ensuring that a higher share of the project benefits is retained in the country. Other benefits of the study have been the lessons learnt by ODA, in particular the need to employ someone with suitable specialised knowledge when drawing up the terms of a commercial contract. The real cause of the maldistribution of benefits was in leaving the Seychelles government to draft and negotiate the cargo handling contract without the benefit of skilled technical advice. Finally it is interesting to note that the wider benefits foreseen for the new port, which can be summarised as a stimulus to the economy, did not materialise. There is a parallel here with roads, which often have the same claim made for them, with the same disappointing result.

Discussion

Mr J. T. Mettam (Bertlin & Partners, Engineering Consultants, Surrey) said that he wished to comment on the subject of ports as he had spent most of his life planning and developing ports. The question of who got the benefits from port development was a fundamental and difficult one. In his experience the main benefits either took the form of a reduction in the time ships spent in ports or an avoidance of potentially costly congestion in the future. It was usually possible to increase port charges but seldom to the point where the increased revenue equalled the cost of the improvement. Because of this his firm had sometimes argued that estimated ship timesaving benefits should be halved when doing appraisals of port development projects because the developing country was unlikely to be able to secure a higher proportion of the benefits than that.

He was critical of the EVSUM Summary of the Port Victoria Project in the Seychelles which he said omitted an important point in the evaluation report, namely that the original development was done in considerable haste without a master plan being prepared for the development of the port. Twenty years ago he had been involved in a port project with the World Bank and it had insisted on a master plan being prepared concurrently with the proposed specific piece of development. The plan justified the latter but in addition it led to significant changes in subsequent investments such as railway tracks and the layout of buildings. He would single out two aspects of the Port Victoria Project which were open to criticism: the dredging, which seemed to have been carried out in the wrong place; and the layout of the buildings which did not allow enough space. If a master plan had been prepared these mistakes might have been avoided. The moral was that before deciding on port investments one should look at least 20 years ahead because once a quay or a breakwater had been built it was there for a very long time.

Mr F. G. Holder (Director, Evaluation Service, United Nations/Food and Agriculture Organisation (UN/FAO) World Food Programme (WFP), Rome) said that his organisation had not been involved in the larger and more sophisticated roads, only the smaller access roads, but he wanted to emphasise that in many situations, especially in mountainous areas, the development process could not start at all without a road. Materials for forestry or soil conservation projects could not be got to the site unless a road was built. One could hardly count the cost of the road because it had to be there—only when it was put in could other benefits begin to flow.

Once a road had been installed the change in the transport mode, eg from porters' heads to the back of a mule or to a four-wheel-drive vehicle, dramatically reduced the cost of living for the essential items. Previously during the rainy season it may have been impossible to get any supplies through for three or four months at a time.

Dr M. Lipton (Institute of Development Studies (IDS), University of Sussex) said he was worried about what happened to the head-loaders once the road went through. Presumably a lot of head-loaders, who were very poor people, would lose their employment. Of course it could be that they were finding other and better sources of income so there might be a gain all round, but if not the road could have made the poor people poorer. These were issues that the evaluations had to address. In the same context he said that he had been fascinated by the West Malaysia Highways Study where the 55 per cent of poorest people were getting only 10 per cent of the project benefits, and where most of the benefits were in the form of time-savings for people who were better off. Would the time saved be spent on production (and if so would this displace labour or would it add to total employment) or on leisure? He wondered if a similar situation might exist with regard to some recent African proposals for long distance roads under some of the South African Development Co-ordination Conference (SADCC) proposals.

Mr J. L. Hine (Transport and Road Research Laboratory (TRRL), Crowthorne) agreed that the question of what happened to poor people who lost their jobs because of a new road was an important one. He said that research had shown that one ten-ton lorry could do the work of 2000 or 3000 head-loaders. On the other hand he quoted the evaluation of roads in Nepal, carried out by a team from the University of East Anglia, which showed that quite unexpectedly wage rates actually increased after the roads had gone in. Other studies had indicated that this had also occurred elsewhere. In Madagascar a study showed that after a new road had been built into a very remote valley about 100 km from the port very significant increases in agricultural production took place and presumably there was a switch from portering to agricultural work. These relationships needed to be explored further.

As to roads intended for the carrying of heavy traffic he suggested that a standard joke amongst transport planners was that no consultant was ever likely to recommend that a road should not go ahead. It was all too easy to fudge the decreases in vehicle operating costs, to lengthen the planning time-horizon, to assume increases in the traffic that would be generated, and to invent agricultural production benefits when these might not exist. The consultants were always under great pressure to come out with positive recommendations. However, evaluations might not throw much light on this issue, because there were still many uncertainties at the time when the evaluations were made. A three-week evaluation was not going to enable a proper study to be made of changes in vehicle operating costs, so a large area of uncertainty was bound to remain. Perhaps the biggest unknown of all was what might have happened if the road had never been built. Long-term research was essential if the answers to some of these questions were to be obtained. As to the implications for future consultancy assignments, Mr Hine suggested that consultants should be asked to do a job that they were well equipped to do, ie to rank alternative schemes using a common methodology—this would be better than asking them simply to appraise a pre-selected project.

Mr A. A. Kingshotte (Evaluation Department, ODA) referred to the evaluation of a road in Kenya which, nine years after it had been built, was carrying a much higher density of heavy lorries than had been assumed at the appraisal. Could not one inference be that in fact the road had been over-engineered and over-expensive in the light of the original traffic forecast?

Mr T. P. O'Sullivan (T. P. O'Sullivan and Partners, Consultant Engineers) raised some questions on the evaluation methodology. He agreed that it was often difficult to find significant benefits from rural roads but that was because the road itself was only one component of a whole package of necessary inputs. It was very difficult to isolate the contribution of the road *per se*. It simply had to be seen as a necessary part of the whole package. This led him to question to what extent cultural and sociological factors had been taken into account in the evaluations. He quoted recent experience with two projects, one in

Thailand and one in the Sudan, where there had been highly contrasting results. In the Sudan, where the cash economy was small, the response of the local people to the road had also been small, but in Thailand, which is an entrepreneurial culture, the response had been so enthusiastic that if the benefits had been measured only from the day the road had been officially opened they would already have been severely underestimated, ie a lot of investment had already gone in and land values had already risen in anticipation of the effect of the new road. As to the implications for engineers, he said that it was highly significant that the value of a road project in an area where head-loading was going on was 100 times that of a project where there was already access by vehicles. The implication was surely that much lower engineering standards might well be appropriate. In a recent case in Papua New Guinea, they had used as a standard accessibility by a four-wheel drive vehicle for around ten months of the year. Although this represented shockingly low standards to engineers used to normal situations it still represented a quantum jump in access for the rural community and had had an enormous impact.

Mr W. Bor (Llewelyn-Davies, Weeks & Partners) widened the discussion to cover the broader planning aspects. He saw infrastructural investments, particularly roads, as links between homes and activities; not to cover these aspects, whilst considering roads, was to look at only part of the question. When considering a rural road one would have to look at its effect on rural settlements. If it were an urban road one would have to consider the traffic situation as a whole. Regarding the evaluation of the Bosporus Bridge he found it very strange that it came up with the finding that the engineers responsible for the bridge had not been concerned with the traffic in Istanbul. It was important to know if this happened because they were not asked to do this in the terms of reference or because they simply ignored it. His impression was that infrastructure was too narrowly conceived by the engineers and too narrowly evaluated by economists. He also pointed out that the word 'environment' had not yet been mentioned in the Conference, although all infrastructure projects must affect the environment in one way or another.

Responding to the discussion, *Mrs J. M. White* agreed with those speakers who had emphasised the need for evaluations to take more account of the environmental and sociological factors. She also agreed with those speakers who had pointed out that some roads, notably those that involved a change in transport mode from man to mule or to a vehicle, could have a major developmental impact. She was more concerned however about the vast majority of roads that involved the upgrading of the road surface and where the impact on vehicle operating costs was usually quite small. She pointed out that 90 per cent of the world's population (excluding China) was thought to live within five km of vehicular access. The overwhelming majority of people today were not living in isolated locations waiting for roads to come along and transform their lives.

Dealing with the suggestion that had been made with regard to the Kenya Road having been over-engineered she pointed out that roads were not usually designed for such short periods as eight years. In developing countries a hard-top road was normally designed for about a 15-year period. One could not go along every few years strengthening a road: it would cause too much disruption of traffic. So it was necessary to make assumptions about the growth of traffic over the long-term planning period.

Referring to the lack of a master plan for the Port Victoria Project in the Seychelles, Mrs White said that the timing of that project had been determined by the fact that the dredger happened to be immediately available from the nearby airport project and as it took a lot of time and money to get dredgers to these small islands it had been decided to go ahead. That might not excuse the lack of a master plan but at least it was a contributory factor.

On the question of port charges and how they were fixed and how the benefits were shared, Mrs White said that the port charges had been raised to a level commensurate with other port charges in the region and which seemed to claw back sufficient benefits for the Seychelles islands.

Finally on the question of the low rates of return on rural roads, Mrs White argued that one inference might be that lower engineering standards should be adopted.

References

Ex-post evaluations carried out by ODA

A Roads with Low Baseline Traffic Flows

[1] Baffoe, F. June 1978 'Evaluation of the district road programme in Swaziland'
[2] Tanner, J., Haswell, M. and Smith, A. October 1968 'Feeder road system of Malawi—study of present and future needs'
[3] Transport and Road Research Laboratory, 1976 'Evaluation of the Ethiopian feeder roads pilot project'
[4] Airey, A. 1977 'The role of feeder roads in promoting rural change in Eastern Sierra Leone'
[5] Halcrow Fox and Associates, 1980 'Baseline study of the Songea–Makambako Road, Tanzania'
[6] Blaike, P., Cameron, J. and Seddon, D. February 1977 'The effects of roads in West Central Nepal'
[7] Carpenter, T. January 1975 'The North Malaita Road, BSIP'.

B Roads with Higher Baseline Traffic Flows

[8] Transport and Road Research Laboratory, 1978 'A partial ex-post evaluation of the 1964–68 Nairobi to Mombasa Road Project'
[9] Plumber, A. J. and Dewhurst, S. A. and Njala College, Sierra Leone, March 1980 'Evaluation of Taima–Bo Road, Sierra Leone'
[10] Jackson, B., Simons, A. and Patel, J. May 1980 'Evaluation of Belize Northern Highway, Section A'
[11] Transport and Road Research Laboratory, 1983 'Thuchi–Nkubu evaluation study'.

C Other

[12] Hill, P. G. December 1981 'Synthesis of Rural Road Evaluations'.

D Other Transport Projects

[13] Jennings, A. November 1978 'Evaluation of Bosporus Bridge Project, Istanbul, Turkey'
[14] Mackay, Sir G., Kesson, J. M. and Knowles, J. W. January 1981 'Evaluation of ODA-financed projects to assist Malawi Railways'
[15] White, J. and Harding, A. June 1981 'Evaluation of the Port Victoria Scheme, Mahe, Seychelles'.

Evaluations carried out by TRRL (Overseas Unit)

[16] Hine, J. L. and Riverson, J. D. N. Institution of Civil Engineers' Conference, London, May 1982 'The impact of feeder road investment on accessibility and agricultural development in Ghana'
[17] Hine, J. L. TRRL Laboratory Report No. 1046, 1982 'Road planning for rural development in developing countries: a review of current practices'
[18] Thomas, S., TRRL Laboratory Report SR 777, 1983 'The value of time savings in West Malaysia; car, bus and taxi occupants'
[19] Thomas, S. TRRL Laboratory Report SR 792, 1983 'The value of time savings in West Malaysia: commercial vehicles'.

B3

Technical Co-operation: The Evaluation of Aid-funded Training by Mr A. P. Thomas, Assistant Director, Technical Co-operation Training Department, British Council

1 Background

The British Council's Technical Co-operation Training Department (TCTD) acts as ODA's agent in adminstering the bilateral training element of the British aid programme. The operation is a large and complex one. TCTD is the biggest department at the British Council headquarters and a significant proportion of the resources of the Council's overseas and British regional networks are also devoted to the handling of TCT Study Fellows. During the 1982–3 financial year, there were over 8000 Study Fellows from 107 countries in the scheme and total expenditure exceeded £35 million.

Given the scale of the operation it is natural that there should have been continuing interest in developing a monitoring system to discover whether the objectives of training in Britain were being achieved. During the 1970s there were ODA Training Reviews, supplemented by the activities of individual British Council officers. It was decided in 1978 that there should be a more systematic effort to evaluate the programme and two posts were created within TCTD to form an evaluation unit.

It was felt that the main emphasis of evaluation activity should be overseas and with this in mind, ten British council officers, concerned with the administration of the TCT programme overseas, were invited to participate in a workshop at Easthampstead Park in October 1978. The main recommendations which emerged were:

a That a structured interview was the best means of collecting data

b That responses should be recorded by descriptive, rather than quantitative, means

c That interviews should take place six to twelve months after a Study Fellow's return

d That the employer should be interviewed as well, if possible

e That ideally someone with expertise in the returned Study Fellow's field and someone from the overseas government should be included in the interview panel.

2 Approaches and Methods

The 1978 workshop recommendations have formed the basis for overseas-based evaluation interviewing by our colleagues abroad. However, the British

Council does not wish to restrict itself to only one method of checking on the value of training. Hence there has been a three-pronged approach based on:

Overseas-Based Interviewing

During the first phase (1979–81) a total of 238 interviews were conducted in ten countries. A report was written by Council officers in each of the participating countries and was passed to British Council staff and to the ODA. The findings were brought together in November 1981 in a report *Training and Development* which was widely circulated. Not all of the countries which participated in the first phase were able to continue but others have joined in the second phase which ended in December 1983. As a result of this there should be a further 200 reports from 12 countries. The approach is still broadly that recommended at the 1978 workshop but there have been changes in the methodology. In particular the samples have been biased to provide information on specific fields of training, such as Adult Education, mainly at the request of TCTD's advisers to whom copies of the completed interview report forms are passed. Another innovation has been to inform advisers before the interviews are carried out so that they can ask the interviewers to follow up particular lines of enquiry. In addition it has been found more effective to interview Study Fellows 12–18 months after their return, and finally questionnaires have been introduced for employers where it has proved difficult to interview them.

End-of-Course Questionnaire

Overseas-based interviewing represents a longitudinal approach to evaluation and concentrates on the training experience of an individual who has an opportunity to comment in some detail on how he has applied his training on return. However, it is not feasible to use this method to obtain a general response from the whole range of Study Fellows. That can only be done by the use of questionnaires, but the response rate is unlikely to be satisfactory if questionnaires are sent to Study Fellows a year after their departure from Britain (the response rate to a Colombo Plan questionnaire was only 8 per cent). Hence a major exercise was mounted in 1981 to get all 3500 Study Fellows departing during that year to complete a professionally designed questionnaire on a wide range of topics affecting the success of their training. It was completed by 2800, more than enough to make the results statistically valid, and 159 tables of correlations have been produced. This represents a vast mass of information and one of the main challenges now is to decide what are the most useful conclusions to be drawn from it, bearing in mind that there are always limitations to subjective views obtained before the Study Fellow had returned to his work.

Training Reviews

During recent years the British Council has participated in ODA training reviews in Pakistan, Nepal, India, Sudan, Bangladesh and Indonesia. These have involved a total of 350 interviews with returned Study Fellows as well as discussions with employers, government officials and colleagues overseas. Where possible, they have been conducted as joint exercises with the active participation of officials from the recipient country and they have added a great deal to the Council's stock of information on the value of training.

Other Approaches and Resources

In addition to the three main approaches outlined above, there have been one or two subject-based surveys using questionnaires. Further information has also become available via surveys conducted by other organisations (eg the Colombo Plan Bureau and the East African universities).

3 Findings and Results

At the conference of Special Course Directors in 1982, Dr Cracknell pointed out that if aid managers were doing their job well it was unlikely that evaluations studies would reveal major shortcomings in programmes. It is therefore reassuring to be able to report that few TCT Study Fellows felt that their training was wasted. Most believed that they were placed on the right course, that they were well taught and that they had acquired skills and knowledge which they were able to apply on their return home.

In spite of this general satisfaction, however, evaluation studies have revealed a considerable number of areas for concern:

a Within the larger programmes there is a need for the nominating ministries to have more coherent plans for overseas training. Too many Study Fellows are still nominated for, and placed on, a specific course which happens to be known to the overseas government, when a more appropriate alternative may be available

b The information flow during the placing process needs to be improved. It has become evident from Study Fellows' responses that the A2 nomination forms do not always describe the training needs clearly; that TCTD sometimes fails to inform the overseas post of progress in placing; and that advisers and institutions do not always deal with applications quickly enough. Most notably it has been reported in virtually every evaluation study that few Study Fellows receive adequate information about their course before their arrival in Britain (although they are generally well-briefed on living conditions)

c Although most Study Fellows are satisfied with the training they receive in Britain, there was a widespread desire for more practical attachments, site visits etc. There was also criticism of some courses for not having a homogeneous enough group of participants

d Accommodation was most frequently cited as a cause for dissatisfaction when Study Fellows were asked about living conditions

e There was almost no complaint about having too much pre-course English language tuition but a significant number of Study Fellows said that they would have liked more

f A number of Study Fellows were transferred soon after their return to jobs where they were unable to use the skill that they had acquired. Others reported that they had been trained at inappropriately high levels of technology. It has also become clear that employers often do not know enough about what the returned Study Fellow learned in Britain because the Course Director had failed to complete the final report, or completed it inadequately g It has emerged that there is a largely unfulfilled demand for follow-up to training in such areas as the provision of journals and small items of equipment, advice from lecturers etc.

4 Implementation and Feedback

It is self-evident that the resources put into evaluation can only be justified if they lead to improvements in the management and administration of the programmes. In some ways this is the most difficult part of the process because of the need to change the behaviour of so many different people. The British Council Representative is a key figure in this and part of the rationale for the overseas-based model of evaluation interviewing was that the evaluator would also be the person most able to bring about change. With his continuous contact with the nominating governments, the British Council Representative is, for instance, in the best position to persuade them to draw up coherent training plans and particularly to discourage applications for specific courses. TCTD has revised the Compendium of Training Courses and in reissuing it has asked that copies should not be passed to nominating governments. Instead, a more general descriptive booklet outlining training opportunities in Britain has been produced so that nominating governments can have some idea of what is offered when making more general training requests.

In order to improve the whole placing process TCTD set up a working party during 1982. Among the recommendations that are now being implemented are:

a British Council Representatives are being advised to discuss training applications with nominees' employers and to return A2 nomination forms which do not give a clear description of the training required. The A2 form itself has also been redesigned to make its purpose clearer and to ensure that it elicits the information needed by advisers

b A new self-carbonating placing pro-forma has been designed. In future, whenever a British Council regional office is asked to place a prospective Study Fellow, this information will automatically be copied to the Representative overseas. At the same time, information about the course will be sent so that the prospective Study Fellow and his employer will be able to judge whether the training proposed will be suitable

c TCTD is also redesigning the interim and final report forms. The main purpose of the latter will be to provide a description of the training programme followed by the Study Fellow and to ensure that employers know what skills have been acquired in Britain.

ODA and TCTD are together trying to ensure that evaluation findings are widely publicised among Course Directors. This is being done by means of special meetings and particularly at the annual Conferences of the Special Course Directors and the Association of Teachers of Overseas Education. It is, of course, appreciated that some of the evaluation findings, such as the unsatisfied desire for more practical attachments and site visits, cannot easily be met. However, it is important that Course Directors should have an opportunity to explain their difficulties as well as taking these points into account in planning future courses.

A number of British Council Representatives are already trying to improve the follow-up service for returned Study Fellows and the Council is considering the possibility of allocating funds specifically for this purpose.

Evaluation findings are also fed into the system in a more routine way. Individual interview reports go to advisers to enable them to build up a picture of the effectiveness of their work. In some cases they also go to the relevant Course Director. In addition sets of interview reports are made available to advisers who are going on tour overseas or visiting institutions in Britain.

Country reports and training review reports do, of course, also go to the ODA Geographical Departments and hence influence training policy as stated in the annual key sheet. It may reassure those who doubt the value of having their programme evaluated that so far the recommendations of training reviews have tended to result in an increase rather than a decrease in the number of awards offered.

5 Conclusion

I am conscious that a paper of this nature raises rather more questions than it answers. The evaluation of a large training programme cannot be a straightforward matter and there are many aspects of training that cannot be quantified. Even when it is agreed that there should be change, its implementation involves a chain of people—the nominating government, the ODA, the British Council overseas and in Britain, advisers and Course Directors. We cannot claim to have devised a perfect system and although we believe strongly that we have already obtained much valuable information we expect that improvement of our methodology will be a continuous process. Hence we shall welcome ideas and comments.

Discussion

Mr J. White (Organisation for Economic Cooperation and Development (OECD), Paris) expressed his disappointment that the same conclusions as Professor R. Simons had reached in his evaluation of training some 20 years or so ago were reappearing again and again. This pointed once more to the problem of applying conclusions of evaluations in a systematic institutional way. Superficially this was curious because aid agencies tended to be functionally organised so that there was usually a department responsible for training. Why then were the lessons not being diffused? He suggested one reason might be that evaluations of whole activities, like the use of experts or advisers, programme aid, or training, were inherently unsatisfactory because in fact these all comprised very heterogeneous ranges of activities. The only exception seemed to be Food Aid where there was now a fairly solidly established body of knowledge and that must be partly attributable to the fact that Food Aid was a relatively homogeneous type of resource transfer.

Mr M. Whitby (University of Newcastle) took issue with Mr Thomas's opening proposition that there were so many models of the training process that one did not know which one to pick and therefore often no model was used at all. He suggested that progress could be made in the evaluation of training if one had a human capital model in mind—even the British Council, dealing with the training of people from many different countries who were going back to work in a great variety of labour markets, would find such a model useful. First of all one would have to recognise that one was dealing with a long pay-back period—up to 20 years or so—and therefore it was important to find out what impact training programmes were having on career profiles. Secondly the benefits of training, both to the individual and to his country, should be reflected in salaries and in promotion profiles and this should be assessed if possible. Thirdly there would need to be a control group—so that it would be possible to find out what the Study Fellows might have done if they had not been sent for training. One way of tackling this would be to start with applicants who had not been granted Study Fellowships and seeing how they had fared. Alternatively, but this would be more difficult, one could choose a control group from non-applicants.

Dr D. N. F. Hall (Principal Fisheries Adviser, ODA) suggested that a distinction should be drawn between training leading to some specific skill accomplishment, and training of a more basic nature that was intended to provide a foundation on which people could develop their careers. One course Britain provided in fisheries was the Diploma in Fisheries Management at Grimsby College of Technology. This course was a general one aimed at producing fisheries officers. ODA's main aim was to train people to do a job. If they acquired a qualification en route that was their good fortune but it was not ODA's main purpose, therefore such a course was not easy to evaluate—the real criterion was how effectively it had helped the participants to do their jobs. Of course for some particular jobs, eg in the research field, a degree was required. Dr Hall and his deputy tried to visit the trainees once a year and often the same kinds of criticism were made. These arose from the fact that the trainees often did not appreciate why particular subjects had been included in the course. He had to say to them that he often knew better than they did what they were going to need in ten years' time. One of the problems of evaluation on the basis of a Study Fellow's future career was that if he was very good there was a high likelihood that he would be selected by his government for something more important and right outside the fisheries area. One Study Fellow had finished up as a Permanent Secretary! However, many of them had become Chief Fisheries Officers which had been most encouraging.

Another evaluation criterion might be the extent to which the country's fisheries industry as a whole had improved after a number of Study Fellows had been trained. In Malawi for instance where quite a number of people had been trained, substantial development had taken place in the country's fisheries industry and this could be attributed, at least in part, to the ODA's diploma course in fisheries management.

The Grimsby course, after running for 15 years, was now showing some sign of having run out of steam. The number of applications in 1983 had fallen and it might be that the time had come to revise the contents of the course. Dr Lawson for example was planning an Advanced Fisheries Training course for people who had taken the Diploma in Fisheries Management five or ten years previously.

One key factor was that it was the governments of developing countries who sent Study Fellows for training and any evaluation process should concentrate on their views of what was required rather than on the trainees' own views.

Mr J. Jacobs (Freelance Consultant) said that he had read the technical co-operation evaluation with an increasing sense of dismay. It had little to say about in-country or third-country training, little about brain-drain (eg from countries like the Sudan), and contained no comparison of the British results with those of other donors. If this was a true picture of the situation it would seem that the Technical Co-operation Training Department (TCTD) of the British Council had in fact gone backwards since October 1978. But he could not believe that this was the case. He doubted if the paper did justice to what the Council had done in the last five or six years. In 1978 the British Council had called its Conference on Evaluation at Easthampstead Park (which he had attended) and the University of Manchester had published the booklet *The Evaluation of Education and Training Programmes in the UK for Study Fellows from Developing Countries,* of which he had been editor. That document contained more than one would be led to believe existed in the collective knowledge of the TCTD.

As to the question of brain-drain from the Sudan, he regretted that there was still so much ignorance between aid donors on issues of this kind and so little sharing of what little information did exist. He suggested that the TCTD might well apply to itself Mr Thomas's comment that the aim of his Department was 'to make sure that people are always reviewing what they are doing'.

Responding to the discussion, *Mr Thomas* emphasised that the resources of his Department were very limited—one man and an assistant clerical officer. They just did not have the resources to pursue the kind of long-range research favoured by Mr Whitby—perhaps it could be mounted as a joint exercise with an academic institution?

As to the fisheries training, and Dr Hall's point that the adviser usually knew better than the Study Fellow what was useful training and what was not, Mr Thomas agreed and said that it was for this reason that the British Council and ODA aimed to interview the employers of the Study Fellows who had returned to their countries whenever they had the opportunity.

As to the points Mr Jacobs had made about the Sudan, Mr Thomas accepted his criticism that the British Council may not have been well informed about the brain-drain from that country, but he said that the British Council's brief was only to evaluate aid-funded training, not to carry out academic studies covering other fields.

B4

Programme Aid
by Mr B. P. Thomson, Economic Adviser, Evaluation Department, ODA

ODA's Evaluation of Programme Aid has been chosen to illustrate the role that evaluation work can play in helping to develop management policy.

Background

Programme aid forms part of ODA's non-project financial assistance to developing countries. It provides finance for British exports, particularly spare parts and other badly needed recurrent supplies, usually in response to balance of payments difficulties.

The importance of programme aid is demonstrated in Table 1 (page 84). It represented between a fifth and a quarter of all British bilateral aid during the 1970s and its significance grew as the decade progressed. However, there was a marked drop in the amount involved from 1980 onwards which was due to the replacement of programme aid to India by aid for projects or sectors.

The character of this form of assistance has been much affected by events in the world economy. In the late 1960s and early 1970s disbursements were dominated by South Asia, especially India. Programme aid was chosen as a means of transferring resources to India because ODA had found difficulty in disbursing tied aid on new investment projects. ODA's good opinion of Indian economic management permitted a policy of few conditions on the way it could be used. However, the international economic climate changed markedly following the first oil price rise in 1973 and this affected the country distribution of ODA's programme aid. Many developing countries, particularly those reliant on primary produce exports, suffered a large fall in their terms of trade. This has posed serious adjustment problems for their economies during the past decade. Programme aid was offered to a growing number of countries to help overcome their pressing balance of payments difficulties and, in particular, to supply urgently needed inputs for agriculture and industry.

Tables 2 and 3 (pages 85 and 86) show the declining importance of ODA's traditional Asian recipients of programme aid and the increasing flow to African, Caribbean and European countries, several of which were previously insignificant recipients of British capital aid (eg Ghana, Mozambique, Zambia, Zimbabwe, Jamaica, Turkey). As a result, the ODA faced a different sort of management problem since some of the new recipients had contributed to their own difficulties by economic policies which failed to promote adjustment to the new situation. There was no generally applicable guidance available for ODA staff seeking to ensure the best use of programme aid particularly when, as in some cases, the recipient government's macroeconomic policies left something to be desired. There was also some unease that programme aid might allow ODA's rigorous investment appraisal

Table 1: The Share of Import Financing* in Gross Expenditure of UK Bilateral Aid (£m)

	1969	1970	1971	1972	1973	1974	1975	1976	1977	1978	1979	1980	1981
1 Import Financing	37.6	58.8	58.6	40.6	34.7	52.4	54.8	72.9	71.5	132.2	171.8	69.9	69.2
2 Total Bilateral	176.9	198.2	242.5	233.3	221.9	266.8	305.2	376.3	387.6	542.1	639.0	604.0	743.0
3 Total Bilateral Financial	133.3	152.6	189.1	171.9	149.3	190.4	208.9	249.0	261.0	389.0	453.6	380.8	526.4
4 (1) as % of (2)	21.3	29.7	24.2	17.4	15.6	19.6	18.0	19.4	18.4	24.4	26.9	11.6	9.3
5 (1) as % of (3)	28.2	38.5	31.0	23.6	23.2	27.5	26.2	29.3	27.4	34.0	37.9	18.4	13.1

Source: *British Aid Statistics*

*The statistics which approach most closely to programme aid are called 'Import Financing' in *British Aid Statistics*. This includes miscellaneous capital goods aid and maintenance aid but not sector aid. Some allocations from the Aid and Trade Provision are also included here.

Table 2: Import Financing by Recipient (£'000)

	1976	1977	1978	1979	1980	1981
Africa:						
Ethiopia	–	–	89	10	–	–
Ghana	–	–	–	6030	10 970	3660
Guinea-Bissau	–	–	1292	–	–	–
Kenya	2150	1032	8562	2816	456	6910
Malawi	–	–	–	–	–	3612
Mozambique	–	2170	2900	1665	1485	1949
Nigeria	470	282	68	–	–	–
Senegal	–	–	–	1000	–	–
Somalia	–	–	810	985	561	144
Sudan	–	–	–	3860	7950	2515
Tanzania	1520	3850	5573	4753	4715	2273
Uganda	–	–	–	760	1117	944
Zaire	–	–	–	–	263	1553
Zambia	–	1960	3835	17 001	4815	4107
Zimbabwe	–	–	–	–	3719	4639
Total Africa	**4140**	**9294**	**23 128**	**38 881**	**36 051**	**32 307**
America:						
Barbados	–	–	–	351	331	130
Chile	4	–	–	–	–	–
Guyana	–	–	5080	300	208	251
Jamaica	–	–	18 880	5690	2816	7444
Total America	**4**	**–**	**23 960**	**6341**	**3355**	**7825**
Asia:						
Bangladesh	2031	7903	16 581	15 541	3622	7365
Burma	131	982	627	509	1123	449
India	61 155	51 581	65 342	103 086	17 551	–
Indonesia	61	2	–	–	–	–
Maldives	45	–	–	–	–	–
Nepal	–	–	–	–	39	–
Pakistan	1341	395	154	872	59	26
Sri Lanka	3999	1299	2355	3177	473	4
Vietnam	–	–	–	3447	–	–
Total Asia	**68 763**	**62 161**	**85 059**	**126 573**	**22 867**	**7844**
Europe:						
Turkey	–	–	–	–	7585	21 185
Total Import Financing	**72 907**	**71 455**	**132 148**	**171 794**	**69 858**	**69 161**

Source: *British Aid Statistics*

Table 3: Share of Total Import Financing (%)

	1976	1977	1978	1979	1980	1981
Africa	5.7	13.0	17.5	22.6	51.6	46.7
America	–	–	18.1	3.7	4.8	11.3
Asia	94.3	87.0	64.4	73.7	32.7	11.3
(India)	(83.9)	(72.2)	(49.4)	(60.0)	(25.1)	(–)
Europe	–	–	–	–	10.9	30.6
Total	**100.0**	**100.0**	**100.0**	**100.0**	**100.0**	**100.0**

procedures to be circumvented. Consequently, a good deal of thought was given to ODA policy and an evaluation was commissioned as part of this in 1979.

Evaluation Study

The evaluation was undertaken in two phases. The first phase reviewed ODA's experience with eight countries: Ghana, Kenya, Zambia, Mozambique, Bangladesh, India, Pakistan and Jamaica. It was a desk study by two ODA economists and concentrated on management issues using data from ODA and Crown Agent's files. The report was produced in August 1980. The second phase looked at the achievement of objectives in more detail. Two field studies, Ghana and Zambia, were specially commissioned by the Evaluation Unit (as it was then called). In January 1983 their conclusions were combined with those of similar studies in Bangladesh and Jamaica into a synthesis of experience with programme aid. With the exception of Bangladesh, all this work was carried out by ODA staff since it was felt that they would be able to address the key issues of management policy more effectively than outsiders.

Evaluating programme aid presents certain methodological problems which became apparent in the second phase. Objectives were generally diffuse and ill-defined. Most programme aid actions had the objective of promoting macro-economic adjustment by supporting appropriate policy measures. In order to evaluate this, the studies had to try to disentangle the influences of government policies and external events on the outcome. For example, if subsequent economic performance was poor was it due to inadequate policies or a further deterioration in the external environment? In practice this proved difficult to say. In addition, there were sometimes preferences for assisting particular sectors or improving the efficiency of firms or parastatals. Evaluating these aspects involved wrestling with the problem of fungibility (ie were the resources provided to the target sectors actually additional to what they would otherwise have received?). During the country

Mr J. K. Wright, Under Secretary, ODA, giving his paper on Feedback.

Dr I. Simpson of Leeds University is interested in the display of EVSUMs (single sheet summaries of evaluation reports) mounted by ODA.

case studies, the evaluators interviewed a considerable number of end-users of the goods provided under programme aid. However, the evaluators lacked the time to look into micro-economic issues in depth and so the interview technique could only give an incomplete and subjective impression of aid effectiveness at enterprise level. There were often political and commercial objectives attached to programme aid. These were even less well articulated than the economic ones and virtually impossible to evaluate as a result.

The Achievements of Programme Aid

The evaluation exercise has been mainly noteworthy for its contribution to the debate on policy within ODA but, in spite of the problems mentioned above, it does have something to say about the effects of programme aid as well. The first phase did not look into the economic consequences in any depth but pointed out that procurement-tied programme aid had seldom proved to be as fast disbursing as expected. On average, it took a year from the date of formal commitment to spend half of each programme aid tranche and two years to spend 80 per cent. The date of formal commitment itself was often some time after the aid had been offered. The reason for delay usually stemmed from the ordering procedure for British goods. This makes procurement-tied programme aid something of a blunt instrument when dealing with urgent balance of payments needs. For example, one study found that the macro-economic impact was attenuated because the peak in aid disbursements coincided with a temporary upturn in foreign exchange earnings as the terms of trade improved.

The four case studies taken in the second phase did not look into the political effects but investigated the economic and, to a lesser extent, commercial consequences in more detail. Three of the programme aid actions reviewed were intended as essentially short-term rescue operations, and were linked to International Monetary Fund (IMF) programmes. In two of them the aid was deemed to be largely ineffective from a macro-economic point of view because the rescue operations failed to influence government policies and the IMF programmes had to be abandoned. The third received a more positive verdict. (The difficulty of evaluating the macro-economic consequences of programme aid is referred to above.) The fourth programme aid action was of a semi-permanent character, reflecting fundamental structural problems in the economy. The evaluation concluded that it would be severely disruptive to the government's development effort if it was curtailed. The studies found that the aid had generally been used effectively by the enterprises concerned and there were no major revelations of abuse or malpractice. There were a few obvious cases where the aid had not been productively utilised, which might have been weeded out by better appraisal. Counterpart funds payments were a problem in some instances because of the debilitated financial circumstances of some parastatal recipients.

Policy and Management Issues

The evaluation has covered a wide range of issues concerned with the appraisal of programme aid, ODA management procedures, procurement, counterpart funds and the like. Perhaps the most important are: the question of objectives, the degree of ODA involvement in detailed spending decisions and the use of programme aid for capital goods imports.

These studies highlighted not only the lack of clear, precise objectives but also the potential conflicts between them. For example, if the primary motivation is political, then the minimum of conditions is likely to be desired. However, there may be a strong economic case, at the same time, for making aid conditional on certain policy reforms. If that proves impractical, the ODA may wish to be involved in the detailed allocation and procurement of goods. The tension between poorly articulated political and economic objectives can mean that neither is achieved: political relationships may be soured by bureaucratic red tape while the aid may be used to put off the day when necessary economic reforms are effected. Alternatively, the commercial pressures may argue for a high proportion of new capital goods orders. This directly conflicts with the need to provide recurrent imports to maintain capacity utilisation during a balance of payments crisis.

The first phase of the evaluation study concluded that ODA stood a better chance of achieving its objectives if programme aid was consistently appraised. Furthermore, the *laissez faire* management policy applied to India appeared inappropriate to the experience of the countries suffering acute balance of payments crises. The study recommended more active ODA involvement to ensure that aid-financed goods are effectively used (eg by approval of end-users as well as restrictions on eligible goods and procurement channels). However, the emphasis changed as a result of the second phase work, which has tended to support the view that such measures are not effective in influencing the overall allocation of resources. As a result, the second phase study concluded that the best insurance of developmental effectiveness was appropriate macro-economic policies. There was also a good deal of evidence, particularly from Ghana and Zambia, that programme aid was most likely to be effective when concentrated on a particular economic sector, when combined with complementary inputs (eg external manpower and investment goods) and when undertaken within a policy framework conducive to economic recovery. This gave support to the view that 'sector aid'* was the best response to the problems of long-drawn-out structural adjustment faced by many less developed countries (ldcs). However, there is a trade-off between achieving effective use of aid at sector level and achieving other objectives (eg rapid disbursement). Consequently sector aid will not always be the answer.

The evaluation discovered a number of cases where programme aid had been used to finance investment goods. This led to questions about whether ODA's appraisal standards were being undermined. However, a more important consideration relates to the economic justification for programme aid. In an acute balance of payments crisis, capacity utilisation in the economy is typically low because of a shortage of imported recurrent inputs. Therefore, scarce foreign exchange should be used to finance essential raw materials and spare parts, not investment goods which may make matters worse. Against that there is the practical consideration that a restriction on investment goods

---

*In ODA parlance, sector aid refers to aid-funded inputs used to support the development of a particular economic sector (eg agriculture or power). It may include aid for manpower, capital goods and recurrent inputs and would be appraised as a package in the light of government policies for the sector concerned.

tends to complicate administration and may lead to delays because of problems of definition.

Feedback

The report of the first phase study was presented in September 1980 at a time when ODA's procedures for programme aid were under active review and the findings tended to confirm views expressed elsewhere in ODA that more systematic appraisal and detailed management intervention was necessary. A number of the study's specific recommendations, eg greater use of appraisal missions, were included in a revision of ODA's internal procedures issued in September 1981. Perhaps the most significant innovation arose from the study's recommendation that programme aid should be subject to approval by senior management committee (in the same way as project aid) in order to ensure adequate appraisal and a consistent approach to implementation. This idea was taken up under the new procedures, and the Projects and Evaluation Committee (PEC) extended its remit to cover programme aid. Incidentally this meant that the same people responsible for considering evaluation studies also looked into proposals for programme aid.

The new procedure also dealt with the sort of goods which should be financed. The emphasis was firmly on maintenance goods; capital goods essentially of a replacement or 'balancing' kind were admissible but other capital goods required thorough appraisal. This coincided with the conclusions of the evaluation.

There was initially some criticism of these new rules from those responsible for managing programme aid, on the grounds that they were unnecessarily laborious and restrictive. It was argued that the maximum discretion is necessary to deal with widely differing local conditions particularly when the ODA is required to take quick decisions as frequently happens in these cases.

As a result, the second phase of the evaluation has coincided with a further policy review. The study basically supported the procedures already in place including approval by the PEC and restrictions on capital goods. This has been accepted but the debate has gone a step further in defining more clearly the role of programme aid in current circumstances.

Programme aid is seen as being essentially designed for short-term balance of payments problems. It would usually be provided in support of an IMF programme although ODA would take its own view on the appropriateness of proposed adjustment measures. In this context, rapid disbursement is an essential attribute. This implied the minimum of restrictions, limited bureaucratic intervention and flexible procedures. Where a longer-term aid requirement is likely then sector aid is generally more appropriate. This followed from the belief that aid effectiveness can be improved first by a more systematic consideration of the sector concerned, relevant government policies, and institutional factors than is possible with programme aid or more traditional project aid; and second by combining aid inputs of various types to strengthen the sector's institutions and influence resource allocation priorities. This implies an important role for technical co-operation and preferably a lengthy association with the sector concerned.

Appraisals of programme aid are now expected to specify their objectives carefully (whether these are economic, political or commercial) and show how the proposed procedures follow from these. They are also expected to suggest benchmarks which can be used in ex-post evaluation.

Conclusions

The evaluation of programme aid has been rather different from more traditional project studies. Of necessity it has been more wide-ranging and clearcut conclusions on effectiveness have not been possible. However, these studies have played an important role in developing the ODA's policy on managing programme aid. The experience is one of rapid feedback within the office. This has been made possible by the use of ODA staff familiar with the key issues as evaluators, by timing the evaluation work to coincide with the process of policy review, and by the fact that the committee responsible for considering evaluations is also the channel for approving programme aid.

Discussion

Mr T. Killick (Overseas Development Institute (ODI)) said he assumed that programme aid was given in the general case to countries where there already existed an International Monetary Fund (IMF) Stabilisation Programme. However, he was doubtful of the wisdom of ODA confining its programme aid to such countries because of doubts about the appropriateness of IMF policies towards at least some developing countries. Even senior management in the IMF itself shared some of these doubts and felt that within their terms of reference, and the constraints these imposed, they could not deal successfully with the problems of the least developed countries (lldcs). The conditions imposed by the IMF were not wholly appropriate to economic management in such countries. For ODA to confine its programme aid in the general case to countries subject to IMF conditionality was to impart a distortion to ODA's own policies. He wondered if any thought had been given in ODA to possible alternatives.

Secondly, he asked why ODA's economists did not favour the provision of capital goods under programme aid. The aim of such aid was to help developing countries cope with their balance of payments difficulties in ways which minimised the adverse impact on development. If indeed programme aid was going to support a specific programme it would be surprising if that programme did not include a substantial volume of investment. A reasonable level of investment needed to be maintained in an economy. Even in the face of a balance of payments constraint he accepted that priority should be given to things like spare parts and intermediate goods, but he detected an ideological bias in the ODA (or was it the Department of Trade and Industry?) against the use of programme aid for capital goods even though ODA's programme aid to any given country in any one year would typically be a very small proportion of its foreign exchange earnings. It could well be that the country could use Britain's foreign exchange assistance most effectively by buying British capital goods rather than intermediate goods, and it did not necessarily follow from that that industry, or the rest of the economy, would necessarily be starved of intermediate goods and spare parts.

Thirdly, Mr Killick referred to the kinds of lessons that ODA had learned from this evaluation of programme aid. In addition to the lessons about ODA's management of this kind of aid he felt there were lessons of a more macro kind relating to wider aspects of aid policy. He was afraid ODA was being rather timid in looking only for the management lessons and overlooking the latter. For example the evaluation had clearly highlighted the importance of quick-dispersing aid, yet this objective had been difficult to achieve because of procurement tying. Should not the evaluation have raised the question of the appropriateness of procurement tying in the context of programme aid? In short, he was making the general point that ODA's evaluations in the future should concern themselves not only with management issues but also with broader questions of aid policy.

Mr A. Jennings (University of Leicester) said that the justification for programme aid in terms of urgent balance of payments difficulties was not the only possible one. An alternative case could be made on the grounds that donor emphasis on basic needs and rural development had resulted in a heavy call on recurrent expenditure budgets. Thus the problem could be seen as a long-term one rather than as a short-term one, with the responsibility falling not so much on some *deus ex machina* event, like an adverse movement in the terms of trade, as on the donors themselves. If so perhaps the donors should do more to help developing countries with their recurrent expenditure problems.

Mr J. White (Organisation for Economic Cooperation and Development (OECD), Paris) suggested that there was a tendency to use the term 'programme aid' very loosely, ie as anything that was not project aid. However, the evaluation clearly focused on the short-term crisis situation calling for an urgent input of resources linked to the relevant policy options to be looked at in the recipient country. These situations usually involved an IMF Stabilisation Programme or a World Bank Structural Adjustment Loan. The problem however was that one was inevitably drawn into what was in effect a country evaluation and that was notoriously difficult to do. Moreover one had to look at what other donors were doing since the conflict between what the various donors were doing was itself a cause of some of the confusion. Finally, the most difficult problem of all was how to apply the conclusions once they had been arrived at. The usual conclusion was that conditionality had failed. That was alright so far as World Bank Structural Adjustment Loans were concerned, one simply decided to suspend the next tranche, but it was far more difficult for a bilateral donor to do likewise because it was not usually feasible to disentangle political factors from balance of payments and economic ones.

Mr White concluded with an observation about all four papers dealing with evaluation findings. The discussions had focused on issues of substance but he felt they had been too narrowly based on British experience. It would be interesting to know if the British experience had been confirmed by experience elsewhere. This was something that the Development Assistance Committee (DAC) Expert Group on Aid Evaluation was attempting to do. The problem was how to organise the vast body of knowledge so as to yield usable results and lessons that were reasonably specific. He had no answers to suggest but this was surely a key issue.

The Chairman, *Mr R. S. Porter (Deputy Secretary, ODA)*, responding in particular to Mr Killick's points, said that so far as procurement tying was concerned one could certainly raise the question but the answer was a foregone conclusion so there really was not much point in pursuing it further.

On the question of including capital goods in programme aid, the usual situation in the developing countries receiving this kind of aid was a vast underutilisation of the existing capital stock and lack of maintenance of that stock. It did not seem very sensible to go on adding to the capital stock in a fairly indiscriminate fashion—it was better to provide the inputs that would enable the existing stock to be utilised more fully. There would be a quicker pay-off and one would be responding to the short-term crisis situation. There was also the subsidiary point that rather careful procedures had been developed for appraising capital aid and ODA did not want to see these being bypassed.

As to the IMF, he agreed that ODA had some philosophical doubts but the right place for these to be aired was at the IMF Board level when particular programmes were being discussed. The situation ODA was anxious to avoid was for ODA's representatives in the IMF to be trying to establish a programme with conditionality built into it whilst someone else in ODA was taking measures that were inconsistent with those objectives.

Responding to the discussion, *Mr B. P. Thomson* took up the question of including recurrent expenditure in programme aid raised by Mr Jennings. He thought the preferred way of dealing with this problem should be through local cost aid although he recognised that there were difficulties. He pointed out that in so far as governments sold the goods received under aid to parastatals, or to the private sector, the result could be a considerable increase in government revenue, ie programme aid could turn itself into a form of assistance towards recurrent expenditure.

As to Mr White's comments he agreed that the evaluation of a specific piece of programme aid was a difficult exercise but it would be even harder if one attempted to look at all such aid to a whole country.

PART

THE EVALUATION SYSTEMS OF OTHER GOVERNMENTS AND INSTITUTIONS

C1
The World Bank
by Mr M. L. Weiner, Director-General
Operations Evaluation, The World Bank

In its efforts to improve its development work, the World Bank has instituted an independent process of assessing the effectiveness of its assistance to member countries. The following paragraphs discuss briefly the nature of this evaluation function and what the Bank's experience with it may suggest for other development assistance agencies and governments.*

Introduction

Operations evaluation in the World Bank aims to provide a systematic, comprehensive, and independent review of the Bank's development assistance experience. Its principal purpose is to help improve the design and conduct of the Bank's future project and non-project assistance. It also enables the Bank to account to its member governments for the results of its finance and advisory support for investments in human and physical capital and for its efforts to help improve development policies, institutions and approaches to development problems.

Assistance to members is evaluated in the first instance against the objective criteria agreed between the Bank and the borrowing country, and secondly, against what would realistically have been expected in the actual circumstances of the project. The evaluations assess experience as perceived by the operational staff, the independent evaluation staff and the borrower. The evaluations seek to assess development effectiveness, not to search for failure, fraud or corruption. The independence of the evaluation staff is assured by their reporting to the Director-General, Operations Evaluation, who is appointed by and reports directly to the Board of Executive Directors. Their work is also subject to continuing oversight by the Board through their Joint Audit Committee of selected Executive Directors.

The Rationale

Since the Bank opened its doors in the 1940s, there has always been systematic 'supervision' (ongoing evaluation) of the projects it assists—to monitor the uses to which Bank funds are put and to follow and assist in implementation. Currently, about 20 per cent of the time of the Bank's operational staff, equivalent to some 435 staff years, is invested annually in the

---

*All references to the World Bank should be read here to include its soft loan affiliate, the International Development Association (IDA), and all references to projects should be read to include non-project assistance. Although most of the Bank's assistance is for development projects, its non-project assistance is also subject to the evaluation process described in this paper.

The first part of this paper is extracted from *Finance and Development*, March 1981: 'Evaluating the Bank's Development Projects', pages 38–40. For further details see *Operations Evaluation: World Bank Standards and Procedures*, second edition, August 1979, available from the World Bank.

supervision of over 1800 Bank-financed projects now underway around the world. The supervision of project implementation is largely concerned with such questions as: Are the monies being spent according to the agreed timetable and for the goods and services intended? Is implementation being managed efficiently and effectively, creating the physical assets intended and generating services as planned? Are the policy and institution-building objectives of the project being realised?

The evaluation of projects after completion adds to these traditional implementation review questions a special concern with benefits. It systematically re-examines, one to two years after disbursements have been completed, the prospects for achieving the objectives for which the expenditures were incurred, in light of the experience with implementation and of such effects as may be visible after completion. Selected projects are also revisited several years later to assess their longer-term impact. Deviations from expectations in the work accomplished and in its cost, duration, and the likely amount and distribution of its benefits are identified, their causes analysed, and their significance assessed. Can successes be replicated? Could disappointments and failures have been anticipated? Can the original objectives be considered in retrospect to have been appropriate? Does the investment remain worthwhile even after taking into account the delays, increases in cost and shortfalls in expected benefits that are often observed? Does the particular experience point to broader lessons for the Bank or for the borrower?

The Process

The Bank's evaluation of project performance is a two-tier process. The first assessment of a project experience and its results is normally made by the operational unit which has managed the Bank's involvement in it. The objective is to have the evaluation carried out in the first instance by those who have been directly involved in the activities being evaluated, so that it may be most useful for future operations. Operational staff record their assessments of experience with all completed projects, without exception. Completion reports are then reviewed by the independent evaluation staff, often on the basis of field visits, for the adequacy and integrity of their evidence, analysis and conclusions, and for the larger lessons they may reveal. Each completion report, normally accompanied by the evaluation staff's performance audit memorandum, is then issued to the Executive Directors and the president of the Bank by the Director-General, Operations Evaluation. Project performance evaluation is thus an integral, but independent, part of the Bank's regular operational activities.

The Bank's borrowers are encouraged to be party to this process. They participate in the Bank's evaluations in two ways: first, by preparing their own post-completion assessments or by collaborating with Bank completion reporting missions when they visit to prepare their reviews; and second, by collaborating with the evaluation staff's performance audit missions and by commenting on draft project performance assessments, which they are invited to do in every case, before the reports are issued to the Executive Directors and the President. Co-lenders are also invited to comment on, and when convenient to participate in, the evaluations of projects they have co-financed.

Until July 1982, all completion reports, when issued, were accompanied by a project performance audit memorandum containing the evaluation staff's independent assessment of the project. These assessments were based on their reading of the completion reports, examination of the files, interviews with operational staff and, in about half the cases, visits with the borrowers and beneficiaries at the project sites. Currently, about 60 per cent of each year's growing number of completion reports are selected for independent performance audit. However, all other completion reports continue to be read by the evaluation staff, sent to borrowers for comment, and then issued by the Director-General to the Executive Directors and the President.

Given the nature of this interactive process, significant dissent by borrowers is unusual. Every now and then, however, agreement on facts may be accompanied by differing assessments of their significance. All such differences are duly reflected in the final reports, and all written comments by borrowers are reproduced as annexes to these reports.

Once each year, the evaluation staff prepare an overview of all project performance audit reports and completion reports issued during the preceding year. Findings are analysed, and patterns of experience and their implications for future operations are identified. This annual review is now regularly released to the general public, in a form identical to that distributed to the Bank's Executive Directors except for the deletion of country and project names. The evaluation staff also manage a continuing programme of special studies—of groupings of projects by sector and/or country, of particular Bank policies and practices, and of the impact of selected projects revisited five to seven years after completion. These special studies offer more searching commentary on aspects of the Bank's operational experience. In recent years, this special studies programme has included over a dozen project impact evaluation reports and broad assessments of experience such as with consultants on Bank projects, rural development projects in Sub-Saharan Africa, water management in irrigation projects, education sector operations, project supervision, delays in project implementation, compliance with loan covenants, and agricultural extension and research.

To date, the evaluation of over 800 completed operations for which the Bank and IDA provided $17.5 billion of finance has revealed that over 90 per cent of these projects were assessed at audit to have been worthwhile for the borrowers, notwithstanding the cost overruns, delays, and the management and implementation problems that many of them encountered. These assessments reflect the re-estimates after completion of the economic return of every project for which such an estimate had been made at appraisal, as well as evaluations wherever appropriate of the institution-building, training, and social and policy effects of each of these projects. These cases underline that critical determinants of project success and replicability are supportive of sector policies, meaningful borrower involvement in the genesis and preparation of projects, and adequate preparation, especially in regard to the appropriateness for local conditions of projects' design and implementation arrangements.

The Borrower's Role

Since the enhancement of borrowers' self-reliance in development management should apply no less to the evaluation of project results than to other dimensions of the Bank's development support, borrowers are invited to examine the Bank's evaluation arrangements, which a number have already done, and to participate in the evaluation process. The objective is to help strengthen national development management by encouraging borrowers to assess for themselves experience with their major investment projects. Whenever available, borrower completion reports on their Bank-supported projects become the primary evaluative document in project performance audit reports. Such borrowers' evaluations are not yet common. It is not easy anywhere, especially in over-extended public administrations, to address the 'what happened and why' questions systematically and forthrightly, especially if evaluation is erroneously perceived to be a high-cost, skill-intensive research activity which poor countries can ill afford, rather than an operational support for government planners and managers. However, many of the politicians and officials now coming to power throughout the developing world are increasingly concerned with the effectiveness of their national development programme. Completion reporting by borrowers is increasing. If present trends continue, ten years from now the Bank's project performance assessments could be based predominantly on evaluations by borrowers rather than on evaluations by Bank staff as at present.

What are the distinctive design features of the evaluation function described above and the highlights of the Bank's experience with them?

The key features may be said to be:

Comprehensiveness: all completed projects are evaluated, without exception

Objectivity: all evidence, analysis and judgement in evaluation reports is subject in every case to at least two-way challenge, and is protected from institutional 'censorship'

Transparency: every evaluation report is issued to all Bank member governments, management and staff, and the evaluation process itself is subject to independent annual evaluation

Participation: self-evaluation by operational staff and borrowers of all project outcomes and feedback of the lessons of experience to new projects is now built into the Bank's operational cycle. This foundation of the evaluation system is continually tested, reinforced and complemented by the independent evaluation staff.

The paragraphs which follow offer brief comment on each of these features.

Comprehensiveness

Operations evaluation in the Bank was not always comprehensive in its coverage. Before the present arrangements developed, the then much smaller evaluation staff concentrated on assessing experience with particular groupings of projects and selected cases for review accordingly. Their reports then constituted the whole of the Bank's formal post-evaluation activity. Operational staff were fundamentally observers; their completion reporting obligations had yet to be established.

Since that early situation resembles what is found today in many places, the Bank's move to comprehensiveness merits special comment.

All of the Bank's member governments, especially the suppliers of its capital, wish now to be kept regularly informed of the effectiveness of its development assistance, as do the President and staff who are responsible for managing it. Without comprehensiveness, overview questions about effectiveness cannot readily be addressed; neither can the incidence and therefore the significance of disappointment or failure readily be known, nor can the adequacy of the Bank's responses to the lessons of its operational experience readily be assessed. The first point to be made about comprehensiveness is thus that with it, the Bank can be accountable on a continuing basis to itself and to its member governments for what it does; without it, it cannot. The frustrations of development assistance ministers who find themselves unable to respond to parliamentary questions about effectiveness must be profound. Disappointment and occasional failure in development are inevitable. But if such cases are not to dominate and thereby distort all perceptions of the effectiveness and management of development assistance, they must be seen in context. Comprehensiveness provides this context.

But comprehensiveness has a cost. Is it excessive?

It would be clearly excessive were comprehensiveness to mean full review of all completed Bank projects (more than 200 annually now) *just* by the evaluation staff. Comprehensiveness became quite feasible, however, with self-evaluation through completion reporting. On-going evaluation (supervision) of all Bank-supported projects was already in place. The introduction of completion reporting by operational staff simply redefined the scope and purpose of their final supervision missions. By doing so, it encouraged staff to anticipate completion reporting questions early so that, when the time came to review the full project experience, a record of significant implementation issues and early evidence of expected benefits would already have been prepared. In this manner, the incremental costs of completion reporting have been kept moderate. During the formative years of comprehensive project performance audit reporting, the evaluation staff 'audited' all completion reports to establish the integrity of this new process. But now that completion reporting has become firmly established and the operational responsibilities for it have been clearly designated, selectivity in performance auditing has become feasible, while preserving intact comprehensive evaluation coverage for member governments and staff.

Accountability to member governments and to the general public is clearly important for a public international agency. But it is not the primary purpose of comprehensive evaluation coverage. Its primary purpose is to help enhance the effectiveness of the Bank as a development institution by requiring *all* operational managers and staff in the normal course of work to confront and reflect upon the results of completed projects. The activities which they manage are not ends in themselves. They have development purposes. Reflecting the Bank's concern with these development purposes, operations managers now have to reassess after completion every *ex ante* justification of Bank assistance against the evidence of what actually happened. They also have to ensure that new initiatives adequately reflect the relevant lessons of the Bank's operational experience.

Objectivity

The most common way of ensuring objectivity is to separate evaluation from operations in order (i) to provide for other views unlikely to be contaminated by concern for 'looking good'; (ii) to ensure that the evidence of results and the methodology for getting and analysing it are appropriate to the circumstances of each project; and (iii) to aggregate and compare case-specific experiences periodically to give context and significance to individual case findings. The Bank's evaluation process seeks to ensure objectivity in all three of these ways.

As far as methodology is concerned, it is regrettable to observe the frequency with which excessive methodological concern for 'scientific rigour' and fear of basing judgement on limited or tentative evidence have had the result of deferring indefinitely the beginning of evaluation work in many agencies. Such concerns have not inhibited evaluation in the Bank. All staff analyses of new projects are required to be as explicit as possible about objectives, means, and expected benefits and costs; they thus naturally define the post-completion evaluation indicators and approach. Evaluation is accepted as requiring informed judgement since most evidence of perform-ance is subject to interpretation, especially when it is incomplete or subjective, as it often is. The goal is, of course, to be as rigorous as time and resource constraints permit, but never to allow the ideal to frustrate the acceptable.

Since even the most 'independent' and 'scientific' of evaluations can provoke debate about the quality and significance of evidence and about whether evaluators' experience has coloured the conclusions they have drawn from the evidence at hand, the Bank's evaluation process provides for at least a two-way challenge to every evaluation. As already noted, three parties, each with a distinct perspective—the operational staff, the evaluation staff and the borrower—are involved in every Bank evaluation. Where operational staff produce the completion report, it is the borrower who comments. Where the borrower produces the completion report, it is the operational staff who comment. The evaluation staff also render independent judgement in every case, on the basis of their own investigations and in light of the comparative experience which they uniquely bring to each case. All significant dissent from evaluation staff findings which cannot be resolved during the discussion of drafts is required to be reflected in the final evaluation reports. The same process applies to all special studies and annual reports, the only exception being that in these cases, borrowers' comments are sought only on their own case studies. Borrowers' comments on reports which are not project-specific are received later, through their Executive Directors, when these reports are discussed in the full Board or in the Joint Audit Committee of the Board.

Transparency

To realise the lesson-learning and accountability objectives of evaluation as effectively as possible, all evaluation reports are made available to all members of the Bank's evaluation 'audience'—member governments, management and staff. Not less frequently than once each year, the major evaluation findings for each sector are reviewed with the sector operations staff for their relevance to the Bank's current operational experience and plans. Wide-spread distribution of evaluation reports enables all members of the evaluation audience to judge whether the evaluation function is being managed in an adequate and cost-effective manner, whether the evaluation questions are significant, whether the methodologies are appropriate, whether the evaluation findings and recommendations are useful and disseminated adequately, and whether the Bank is responsive to these findings. The Joint Audit Committee of the Board, which has oversight responsibility for the function, addresses these questions continually. The Committee discusses all major evaluation reports when issued, and a sub-committee reviews in detail selected project performance audit reports and interviews the evaluation and operational staff who prepared them. Once each year, the Committee reports to the full Board its assessment of the evaluation function. The Committee's findings are discussed at the same meeting at which the Board discusses the Annual Report on Operations Evaluation and the Annual Review of Project Performance Audit Results.

Participation

It will be apparent by now that evaluation in the World Bank is not the task of just the Bank's independent evaluation staff. It is also a responsibility of Bank operational staff. The respective roles of these two parties are clearly specified and complementary. Similarly with feedback and follow-up: operational staff are responsible, but the evaluation staff monitor and report upon its adequacy as they see it.

The role of borrowers is also clearly specified. All borrowers now undertake to prepare completion reports on their Bank-supported projects as the culmination of their other reporting obligations to the Bank. Where borrowers have more than just occasional completed projects coming up for evaluation, operational staff are expected to explore a more structured borrower involvement beyond that of just the project agency, for which they may seek the advice and assistance of the evaluation staff. Some member governments now seek to participate in Bank evaluations as a first step towards establishing their own evaluation function to review other major projects in their development programmes. To encourage such participation, annual reports on operations evaluation now inform the Bank's Board and management of the actual and planned involvement in project evaluation by each borrower government which has five or more completed projects coming up for review in the next 12–18 months.

The arrangements described above reflect a particular institutional experience. They may thus not be fully replicable in other settings. They are also evolving in response to changing constraints and to changing emphases in Bank assistance. Evaluation commentary on completed operations is also changing with the growth in the inventory of evaluated projects. The scope for comparative comment has become much enhanced as over 800 project performance audit reports are now available for reference to evaluation and operational staff and another 200 or so are being added every year. Attention to the institution-building and policy impact of operations programmes is also increasing in response to current operational concerns and to the persistence of performance shortfalls in these areas.

However, neither the underlying objectives of the Bank's evaluation arrangements nor their key design features are institution-specific. All are adaptable to other institutional environments. How evaluation activities are organised and staffed can vary widely. Evaluation can be done by outside consultants, by internal evaluation units or by some combination of the two. Evaluation staff can report to a senior or chief executive officer or to a Board of Directors. Evaluation can be initiated soon after completion, later when impact can be more readily observed, or some combination of the two. The Bank's approach to each of these aspects has evolved. But these features are not the critical ones. What is critical, in this paper's view, is whether or not operational staff also participate in the evaluation process. The Bank has opted for the active involvement of operational staff for the very fundamental reasons noted above. Its experience with this involvement suggests that if operational staff are permitted to remain observers, whether for 'budget reasons', because they are 'too pressed for time' or because 'they can't be trusted', evaluation coverage will remain limited, lesson-learning will be constrained, and the beneficial discipline of managerial accountability for results will have been foregone.

C2

United States Agency for International Development (USAID) by Ms M. Hageboeck, Office of Evaluation, Bureau for Programme and Policy Coordination, USAID

Introduction

The practice of evaluation in USAID (henceforth 'AID') has an extended history. However, prior to the mid-1960s, evaluation was not a systematic process which was well integrated into the overall AID management system. In the 1960s initial attempts were made to make evaluation a normal element of project and programme management. A requirement for evaluation reporting on technical assistance projects was instituted, but the results were found to be less than satisfactory. In 1969 AID undertook a study of its existing evaluation practices and found that many of its difficulties with evaluation stemmed from the fact that its projects did not have clear objectives against which evaluations could assess performance.

The present AID evaluation system was initially installed in 1970 and, based on the results of AID's 1969 examination of its evaluation work, the new system called for the establishment of a basis for evaluation during the design of technical assistance projects. Specifically, it required that project objectives be stated clearly, together with the hypotheses implicit in the project design, assumptions the designers made about conditions in the project environment, performance targets for each major objective and plausible measures of such performance as was hoped for by the designers. Baseline data on these measures was also called for by the new instructions. In 1974 these requirements for establishing a basis for evaluation were extended to additional types of foreign assistance projects administered by AID.

Through the 1970s, evaluation work in AID concentrated on the assessment of performance in projects in terms of the objectives laid out in project designs. The majority of AID's evaluations were focused on projects in which AID was actively engaged. Thus, the emphasis in evaluation reports was on performance in implementing projects and on the very early results which implementation produced. Occasional evaluations tried to go beyond this, including several studies which examined the effects of sectoral programmes in Latin America. However, programme level studies and project level evaluations which could be classified as 'summative' or 'ex-post' assessments were extremely rare.

In 1979, AID initiated a new series of evaluations designed to fill the information gap concerning the impact of AID-funded assistance. This programme again concentrated on project, rather than programme, evaluation, recognising that numerically projects far outweigh programmes and other types of assistance in the AID portfolio. The AID 'impact evaluation'

Dr D. Thornton (Reading University) right and Dr I. Carruthers (Wye College) examining the display panels.

Two Conference participants deciding which of the EVSUMs to select during a break in the Confer

programme was set up to examine a series of projects in a particular field or of a similar type and to draw from several evaluations general lessons which could be applied to future plans and decisions about projects of the type examined by an 'impact evaluation' series. Topics to be covered in this way were to be selected by AID's senior staff. To facilitate the use of findings from these evaluations, which were to be carried out in series rather than simultaneously, AID elected to publish 'impact evaluations' as they were completed, leaving the work of synthesis until all of the evaluations in a series were completed; a task that is proving to take something slightly over one year.

During approximately the same period during which AID has been engaged in its 'impact evaluation' work, other units in AID have begun to engage in studies which have a broader character than the traditional project evaluations carried out during project implementation. Experimental work with comparative evaluations of some of AID's Food for Peace projects has been underway for several years. Retrospective longitudinal studies have been initiated for several countries where AID's work in a particular sector was of long duration. Use of the 'case study' method has been attempted as a means for characterising project effects in projects which have numerous sub-projects, and in 1982 a comparative study of an on-going set of projects in one field was carried out by a regional bureau with the intent of using the study findings to reformulate the bureau's policy and programme in that field. Plans also exist for evaluating the overall effects of AID programmes in particular countries. Overall, it is a period of great experimentation in AID. As these experiments bear fruit, they are certain to affect the structure and scope of the AID evaluation system in the 1980s.

Objectives

The primary objective of AID's evaluation work is to improve the policies, programmes, projects and other types of foreign assistance activities in which we and the developing countries are engaged. The central task of evaluation is to provide an empirical and reasoned basis upon which forward-looking decisions can be based. The true measure of the value of AID's evaluation work is in its utilisation. AID's focus on the application of evaluation findings is specific, rather than general. Evaluations are intended to affect:

a Decisions and actions in on-going foreign assistance activities which improve the probability that those activities will achieve their objectives and that their total effects will be positive from a development perspective

b Broad resource allocation decisions, such that over time AID's resources flow toward the types of assistance which have proven to have positive development impact

c Decisions concerning the planning of future programmes and projects which reflect AID's accumulated understanding of the factors that lead to positive development impact through projects and programmes, and

d The formulation of AID policies and procedures, such that they are effective management tools which support AID's mission.

An important secondary objective of AID's evaluation work focuses on the education of its staff and developing country personnel. Through evaluations, particularly evaluations in which designers of projects and programmes as well as evaluators participate, we seek to promote a greater understanding of the value of experience, the factors which influence project success and the means by which information about project performance is obtained. We believe that it is in the interest of the developing countries to develop their own capacity to evaluate programmes and projects and to utilise that information in forward planning.

Documentation is a by-product of evaluation in AID rather than a central objective of the system. It is, however, a critical by-product. In the absence of documentation on evaluation findings and lessons, it would be impossible for AID to aspire to objectives (b), (c) and (d) above since all depend upon the existence of a retained memory of what AID has learned from its evaluation processes. There are other obvious advantages to having this type of record which while not the primary concern of AID's evaluation system are none the less important. We note in particular that our discussions with the US Congress have been enhanced by our practice of sharing our 'impact evaluation' studies with the various representatives and committees which oversee AID's work. Academic organisations, here and abroad, as well as the contractor and grantee organisations with which AID works are other key audiences for our evaluation reports.

Organisation of Evaluation Work in AID

Consistent with our orientation toward the utilisation of evaluation findings and lessons in forward planning, AID's evaluation system is a decentralised one, with evaluation work and evaluation officers placed close to the locus of decisionmaking. We recognise four primary levels of management decision-making in AID and our evaluation system is built around them. The four levels of management upon which our evaluation activities focus are: project and programme managers, Mission Directors and, in Washington, central bureau Office Directors who oversee a collection of programmes and projects, bureau managers, whose span of administration subsumes the work of a number of Missions and/or Offices, and the AID's Administrator and the senior staff of the organisation, as a group concerned with the full range of AID's foreign assistance work. Responding to this management structure, we have evaluation officers operating at three levels of the organisation:

a Mission Evaluation Officers, whose span includes the evaluation work for projects and programmes and the evaluative work which responds to the needs of the Mission Director. (In Washington, we have an equivalent arrangement in the Offices in our major central bureaux. Thus, for example, there is a designated evaluation officer in the agriculture unit of our Science and Technology Bureau whose work covers both the projects and programmes in that unit and the evaluation needs of the Office Director)

b Bureau Evaluation Officers, who oversee the evaluation work within their organisational unit and manage the evaluation work which responds to bureau level requirements for evaluation information, and

c AID's central Office of Evaluation, in the Programme and Policy Co-ordination Bureau, which (1) manages the AID 'impact evaluation' programme that responds to the evaluation needs of the AID Administrator and the senior staff as a group and (2) acts as overall manager of the AID evaluation system and its central point for the development of evaluation guidance and other methodological and procedural materials.

Supplementing this arrangement of evaluation officers, AID created a central Office of Development Information in the mid-1970s to serve as the repository of AID's accumulated 'memory' of what evaluations and other studies had learned over the years. This central unit has the responsibility for storing and retrieving evaluative information and making it available in a timely and usable form to AID staff, developing country personnel who work with AID, contractors and grantees and others who have a need for this information.

While the responsibility for managing evaluation work and for retaining such information as that work produces lies with AID's evaluation staff and with the Office of Development Information, the responsibility for utilising evaluation findings and lessons is more broadly distributed across AID's staff. The primary responsibility for utilisation lies with the AID officers who actually plan, budget, manage or administer and implement the US foreign assistance programme. In other words, it is to those officers who work with projects, serve as Mission and Office Directors, Assistant Administrators at the bureau level and the AID Administrator that the primary responsibility for utilising evaluative information in forward planning falls.

As a means of connecting the evaluation and 'memory' functions with the responsibility to utilise evaluation findings and lessons, AID has established requirements for the utilisation of evaluation information in the design of projects and programmes, in the preparation of country development strategies and annual budget submissions. In 1982 and 1983 we strengthened several of these requirements and during the same period we began an effort to more systematically review compliance with these requirements.

The Relationship of Evaluation to Appraisal, Monitoring and Audit

In AID we distinguish evaluation from appraisal on a timewise basis. We use the term 'appraisal' to connote those preparatory and pre-investment assessments we make prior to funding a project or programme or adopting a policy or procedure. The term 'evaluation' is reserved for assessments undertaken after a project, programme or other type of foreign assistance activity has been funded, either during the implementation period for the activity or on an ex-post basis.

Monitoring procedures for keeping track of the substantive progress in a project or programme in terms of its plans as well as its schedule and resource use budget is the responsibility of the unit within AID which administers a project or programme. Our different bureaux employ slightly different practices in this area and below this level there are different patterns in our various Missions and Offices which conform to the general monitoring scheme utilised by the bureau of which they are a part. Through much of the 1970s, the work of monitoring and the work of evaluation was quite intertwined, with a good many evaluation exercises consisting primarily of a summarisation of monitoring information. In part this overlap was stimulated by then existing evaluation requirements which called for 'annual evaluations'. These exercises, which proved very useful to many of our Missions which viewed them primarily as opportunities to review and tighten management procedures for projects, did not, as our late-1970s reviews of our evaluation holdings demonstrated, yield the types of information we sought from evaluation work. By 1980 we had begun a concerted effort to separate our monitoring and evaluation work, thus enhancing both by letting them better perform their separate tasks. We eliminated the requirement for 'annual evaluations' quite early on, but in practice we found that Missions were still scheduling these 'annual' events as late as 1981. Through a major shift in our evaluation planning procedures, we have now begun to eliminate what are in effect annual monitoring reviews from AID's evaluation programme, while at the same time encouraging our Missions to continue this practice as they deem appropriate within their monitoring programme.

Audit in AID is distinguished from appraisal, monitoring and evaluation work primarily by the individuals responsible for this work. Appraisal, monitoring and evaluation are all tasks which are carried out by the regular staff of the organisation, operating in its several bureaux. Audit, on the other hand, is the responsibility of the staff of AID's Inspector General, which reports directly to the AID Administrator. The scope of audit work includes both the traditional audit functions and, since 1972, the examination of the results of foreign assistance activities. The introduction of a concern with results into the guidance and legislation governing the work of the Inspector General's unit has meant that to some degree this unit examines some of the same issues that are examined within the main structure of the organisation through monitoring and evaluation. The coverage of audit work is however limited. From the point of view of the US government some overlap between monitoring and evaluation by an agency's management and independent review by the agency's audit staff is desirable. The monitoring and evaluation work done by an agency's management is considered to be the basic means by which agency programmes are self-correcting and self-improving. Audit provides an agency's Administrator with an independent check on the programme and on the effectiveness of these internal improvement systems. Overall, the functions are viewed as being complementary.

Coverage of AID's Evaluation System

In principle, AID's evaluation system applies to all the work carried out under the US foreign assistance programme: projects, country level programmes, 'non-project' assistance within country programmes, programmes administered by AID's central bureaux, AID policies and procedures and such other actions as we undertake. In practice, our evaluation coverage is not complete, largely as a function of the level of effort required to move from our current volume of evaluation work to a more complete coverage, but partly as a function of methodological limitations and of our recognition that there is a trade-off between quality and quantity in evaluation work.

In 1981 we began monitoring the coverage of our evaluation work more closely than we had in the past. By comparing evaluation schedules submitted by the Missions and Bureaux with actual evaluations completed during a fiscal year, we found that we were, as an agency, completing roughly 45 per cent of the evaluations we planned in any given year. As noted above, 1981 was the year when we began to actively discourage the inclusion of annual monitoring reviews on evaluation schedule submissions. As of 1983 we are beginning to see the results of these instructions and of our effort to monitor and feedback information on the degree to which our Missions and Bureaux carry out the evaluations they plan. For the Financial Year 1983 (FY83) our per cent completion rate was approximately 65 per cent and we have set a completion rate target of 75 per cent for Financial Year 1984. Through these combined actions we are beginning to discourage *pro forma* scheduling of evaluations, encouraging instead the scheduling of evaluations which respond to information needs associated with up-coming decisions. Simultaneously, we are seeing improvements in AID's commitment to carry out the evaluations it schedules.

We are currently engaged in a retrospective effort to determine what our actual coverage of the AID project portfolio has been since we began keeping evaluation reports in the Office of Development Information. Our current rough estimate is that over the years since 1974 when we began keeping such records, our evaluation work has addressed between one quarter and one third of AID's entire project portfolio. The retrospective analysis of coverage, which we expect to complete this fiscal year, will help us understand whether the evaluations we have undertaken have concentrated on/ignored specific types of AID projects or whether our coverage has been, in effect, 'random'. If the coverage has been skewed in a noticeable way, we should be able to take corrective steps in future year evaluations based on the findings of this review.

A factor which is beginning to interact noticeably with evaluation coverage is one we will call 'absorbtive capacity' for want of a better term. We now have a significant number of evaluations in our Office of Development Information 'memory' bank and an even larger number of project designs, with their preparatory analysis materials. A collection of this nature quickly becomes unusable in the absence of procedures for summarising and synthesising its contents. Since 1979 we have been engaged in efforts through the Office of Evaluation to identify the 'patterns' of findings and lessons in these evaluations, primarily as a first step in our 'impact evaluation' work, but also in response to other needs. The work we are now doing corresponds to some of the work done in 1976 by the Office of Development Information, which even then demonstrated that on any given topic, AID had a vast store of information. At present we are conducting a number of experiments in what American evaluators call 'meta-analysis' or the synthesis of evaluation findings from evaluation studies which were not undertaken using methodologies that facilitate cross-study comparisons. Synthesis work under these conditions is extremely difficult, as one exercise which was undertaken by donor organisations through the evaluation committee of the Organisation for Economic Cooperation and Development's (OECD) Development Assistance Committee (DAC) has demonstrated to all of the DAC donor organisations. Difficult problems in this area, which AID is now addressing, are demonstrating that coverage alone is an inadequate measure of the quality and utility of an evaluation system. Thus, during the next several years we anticipate significant work in this area rather than on expanding the numerical or per cent coverage of our evaluation work, at least with respect to project evaluations. In the area of programme and policy evaluations, by contrast, coverage may well increase over the next several years.

Evaluation Planning and Timing

The planning of AID's evaluation work, including the selection of projects, programmes and other activities to be evaluated and the timing of evaluations proceeds in several stages in AID. These stages are most complete with respect to projects. Gradually they are being instituted for other types of AID work.

a Evaluation Planning During Project/Programme Design

Since 1970, when AID installed its current evaluation system it has required the preparation of two elements of a project design which pertain to evaluation. As the system has expanded to cover additional types of projects and some of AID's programmes these requirements have followed:

1 A Basis for Evaluation

As stated above, all project designs are required to provide a basis for subsequent evaluation in the form of clear objectives, hypotheses concerning the development results project actions will produce, assumptions about conditions in the project environment upon which success depends, performance indicators and targets for all major objectives and methods for securing information on performance in terms of the project's objectives. The technique AID uses for organising this information in project designs is called the 'Logical Framework', which is both a way of thinking about projects and a matrix for recording the key elements of a project design which constitute the basis for its evaluation. As suggested by particular projects, baseline data against which later changes can be assessed is called for as well.

Over the years, AID has noted several problems with the utilisation of its techniques for establishing a basis for evaluation including:

i A tendency on the part of designers to state the logic of the design and the performance measures *after* they have designed the project, rather than as part of the process. This results in products which are not terribly clear or well developed and which have limited use as evaluation guides

ii A tendency to treat 'assumptions' casually during the design process. Evaluations have now shown that for many projects 'assumptions' are a major source of difficulty during implementation and in terms of achieving intended impact

iii A *pro forma* use of the idea of a hierarchy of objectives embodied in the 'Logical Framework' approach* combined with a tendency to try to express the connection between the project and a sectoral or national objective within a four-level hierarchy of objectives. The result here is something we are calling 'jamming'—efforts to put too many objectives into too few stages of logic and/or the omission of steps in a project logic. Several years ago AID suggested to designers that it was very legitimate to expand the 'Logical Framework' matrix horizontally to make room for additional objectives. We are now beginning to

*The 'Logical Framework' is an approach which AID uses during project/programme design to specify the objectives in a project/programme, articulate its development hypotheses, the key assumptions upon which project/programme success depends, verifiable indicators of project/programme performance and means of verifying whether the target levels for these performance indicators have been realised. The 'Logical Framework' is expressed in a simple matrix once the elements of the project logic have been thought through. It is also used as the basis for subsequent evaluation work.

make that suggestion more forcefully in design reviews where we encounter 'jamming'

iv 'False promises' with respect to either baseline data or such control groups as designs indicate will be established and maintained to provide a basis for measuring key dimensions of performance. Evaluations, particularly our 'impact evaluations', are demonstrating that in practice these promises are rarely kept. We are simultaneously experimenting with post-facto approaches to reconstructing baseline information, including using developing country record-keeping systems where they exist, and ways of narrowing the range of variables on which it is essential to have baseline data or control groups in order to later measure change. In addition we are attempting to determine the feasibility of utilising information we maintain on a range of development indicators in AID's Social and Economic Data Service data bases as a substitute for baseline and monitoring data secured at the project level. The outcome of these experiments will influence the direction we take with respect to requiring that projects make good their promises with respect to this type of information.

2 Design Stage Evaluation Plans

At this point in time, the design stage evaluation plans for AID projects generally identify only appropriate times for undertaking evaluations during the active life of projects. The suggested timing of such evaluations is to some degree based upon expectations concerning the occurrence of specific events in the project, eg if the project is agricultural or educational in nature timing may be linked to the end of a farming or school cycle. While the suggestions provided in these plans for the timing of evaluations are consistent with AID guidance on 'appropriate' timing, the evaluation plans often need to be updated as the project evolves, particularly when they state the specific month rather than the event which should trigger evaluation work.

From an evaluator's perspective these plans are turning out to be of very little use. At the same time, we are beginning to recognise the importance of having project designers identify the questions and issues they believe should be addressed in evaluations of the projects they design. Their expectations concerning the evolution of the project, problems it will encounter, assumptions they made during design which they feel will need to be rechecked by evaluations are all observations which we now feel will be of greater use to evaluators than are the rough schedules which now appear in project designs as an evaluation plan. We are currently revising our evaluation planning guidance for project designers along the lines suggested above. The new guidance in this area will focus on:

i Event-oriented schedules, going beyond the active life of the project as well as covering points for evaluation during AID's implementation period

ii Issues/questions to be raised by evaluations, tied to the suggested timing of evaluations

iii Additional discussion/attention to the alternative ways of assessing performance, including an expectation that the designer will identify existing data series and record-keeping operations as well as suggest baseline and control group procedures, weighing each option in terms of cost and probability that it will actually be a usable basis for making comparisons during subsequent evaluations.

b Annual Evaluation Plans

AID's long-standing requirement for annual evaluation schedules from its Missions was revised and expanded in Financial Year 1981 (FY81) to focus on the forward decisions the Missions planned to make which would be facilitated by evaluative information. This 'decision-driven' annual exercise is now being used by AID to cull from project evaluation plans, the Mission's country development strategy and other sources those information needs which actually require attention during the next two fiscal years. We are moving rapidly in the direction of scheduling only those evaluations we intend to utilise. For some projects this will mean ignoring the suggested timing of design stage evaluation plans; for others it will mean moving those schedules forward, or supplying them where they were not prepared adequately. As suggested in preceding sections of this paper, we believe that the changes we are making in our annual evaluation process will improve the linkage between evaluation studies and their utilisation. The refinements we intend to make in design stage evaluation plans fit in with these changes. The reduced emphasis in design stage plans on scheduling and the increased emphasis on evaluation questions and measures should improve the utility of these early plans by making them valuable whenever real needs indicate that an evaluation of a particular project is timely.

c Agency-Wide Evaluation Plans

As of FY81, we instituted a process for creating an Agency-wide evaluation plan on a fiscal year basis. The intent of this plan was to subsume Mission level plans, understand them as a whole and then add to them our plans for bureau-initiated and 'impact evaluations'. To date we have published only the FY81 plan. The FY83 plan is now being prepared, and while we did not finish our preparation of the FY82 plan in the relevant time frame we may back up and complete it just to keep this new series in order. The timing of these first few Agency-wide plans has been difficult, since we used a late cycle for preparing the annual evaluation plans at the Mission level—a needed relaxation of our normal spring timing of this requirement allowed in order to make the shift in the type of plan we were requesting. As of this spring, annual evaluation plans will again be required from the Missions in May, making it feasible to complete bureau level and 'impact evaluation' planning prior to the end of a fiscal year with an eye to publishing the Agency-wide plan at the start of each new fiscal year. Through our exercise of creating an Agency-wide plan, we hope to be able to identify economies in our evaluation work as well as avoid unnecessary duplication of effort at the different levels at which this work is undertaken.

Evaluation Teams, Reports and Quality Control Procedures

As the preceding sections suggest, AID is becoming increasingly aware of the quality and utility of its evaluation work. This awareness is leading us in new directions which are designed to improve the impact of AID evaluation activity in our forward programme. Much of this work is leading us back into the way we conduct our evaluations. As has already been noted, the scope of past evaluations and the issue of comparability have surfaced as areas requiring attention. Working with the users of AID evaluations, we are also becoming aware of the fact that evaluators do not always write in ways that are easy for readers to use—by and large evaluation reports are too long, lack executive summaries and fail to state the conclusions as sharply as readers would have them stated. We are also aware of the fact that in our Office of Development Information we are spending an enormous amount of time abstracting reports which could be better abstracted by their authors.

1 Evaluation Teams

Over the years, AID has been able to do a reasonable job of recruiting skilled experts in specific fields for evaluation teams. In our 'impact evaluation' work we have been able to recruit senior personnel from the agency as team members. In our mission and bureau evaluations we have been able to access experts from the United States as well as from the developing countries for evaluation teams. Yet as we look back over our evaluation work, we have not taken as complete advantage of these resources as we might have. The 'missed opportunities' for conducting higher quality and more useful evaluations appear to stem from a number of sources:

a Insufficient attention to evaluation 'scopes of work' from a substantive perspective, including poorly stated evaluation questions, the absence of needed background on the original design and current status of the project, the absence of information on the status of baseline and other sources of data upon which evaluators could base their work, etc

b Inadequate attention in 'scopes of work' and in solicitations to bidders on evaluation studies on the development of an evaluation strategy, methodology, plan for analysing data, etc, which *de facto* has resulted in rigorous and comparative methods being applied only where the evaluators themselves put a premium on this type of preparation or responded well to the occasional request for this type of preparatory work in our solicitations

c Inadequate attention given to team preparation and management and inadequate time allowed within evaluation study frameworks and budgets for (a) adequate 'homework' on existing reference materials on the project, (b) sufficient briefings and discussions of evaluation objectives with pertinent parties in Washington and overseas, both in our Missions and with the developing country, and (c) inadequate time for data analysis and interpretation after field work is completed.

All of these problems in the preparation for an execution of studies stem from a premium placed on 'getting on with the job', usually in response to urgent needs for the findings of the evaluation studies. Hopefully, the improvements in evaluation planning procedures described above along with other work on these areas will begin to temper the 'rush to the field' with an understanding of the compromises that unwarranted speed toward data collection often entails.

2 Evaluation Reports

In 1970, when AID installed its current evaluation system it initially conceived of evaluation reports as reports on an evaluation *process* carried out by a Mission. The reporting format featured decisions resulting from the evaluation on the first page, followed by a synopsis of the evaluation findings organised according to the terminology of AID's 'Logical Framework' and the key ideas which supplemented that terminology such as 'unplanned effects' and 'lessons learned'. Over the years, submission of the full evaluation report which stood behind this process summary was *ad hoc* for the most part, some coming in with copies of the full reports, others not. In other cases, we found that the outline provided for preparing an evaluation summary was being used to write a full report and what we were receiving lacked a summary. In the years in which AID's primary focus for the utilisation of evaluation results was on improving ongoing projects in the Missions this type of reporting was adequate. Today, as we are moving to use evaluation findings and lessons as the basis for planning new projects and programmes, broad resource allocation decisions and policy formulation, a different concept of evaluation reporting is needed.

Through current experiments in our 'impact evaluation' programme and in our bureaux, we are examining the nature of our evaluation reporting needs. Our 'impact evaluations' currently incorporate both a summary of 'lessons learned' and a more complete report, with detailed annexes, in one volume and are supplemented by a synthesis of the studies in a series whenever a particular series is completed and reviewed through a conference which calls together managers and experts in the particular field. In our Africa Bureau, we are currently calling for summaries of evaluations which focus on 12 questions which are designed to pull out information about the approach to and degree of 'technology transfer' achieved. Our Asia Bureau is experimenting with an approach to evaluation summaries which more closely resembles the conventional executive summary that accompanies many evaluation reports submitted by outside contractors. Internal reviews of these variants on our general requirements for evaluation summaries are suggesting that there are a number of common or fundamental elements which all incorporate and which may constitute the basis for a revision of our reporting requirement. As suggested above, we are also actively discussing the idea of having authors of evaluation reports prepare abstracts which conform to a format our data bases will accept and use for long-term storage and retrieval purposes.

While these experiments are leading toward requirements for evaluation reports as contrasted with reports on the evaluation process, we value the inclusion of information on decisions taken as a result of evaluation reviews in our Missions and Bureaux and intend to retain that process feature of our evaluation reporting requirements. In addition, we are recognising the potential value of having the recipients/users of evaluations comment in the evaluation summaries concerning their perceptions of the value and utility of evaluation studies. As we continue with our experimental work in 'meta-analysis' or synthesis, we may find that additional changes in our evaluation reporting procedures can help facilitate the later use of findings from individual project and programme evaluations. Already we see the potential for gaining knowledge about issues that cut across types of projects, eg recurrent costs, participation, etc, by calling for reporting on these matters, at minimum, in our future 'impact evaluations'.

3 Quality Control and Feedback

The American actor, Humphrey Bogart, was reported to have once said that the only truly fair way to distribute awards for cinema performances was to require that all nominees for superior acting awards be filmed playing the same part. The problems inherent in recognising quality in evaluation have the character of which Bogart spoke. Nonetheless, we along with the Academy of Motion Picture Arts and Sciences are now prepared to take on the job of judging quality. Recognising that over the years we have done little to sort out high quality evaluations from those which met low standards or to provide feedback and guidance to those who conduct or manage evaluations, we began in 1981 to operationalise the concept of 'meta-evaluation' or evaluation of evaluation in AID. Initial work in this area has shown that by examining evaluation reports we can at most judge the technical quality of evaluation work. We cannot, from reports alone, judge their true value which lies in the utilisation of their findings and lessons. The 'meta-evaluation' system we have developed will be used primarily to diagnose problems in our evaluation work and to prepare new and supplementary guidance for our staff. The system rates evaluations on such factors as whether they stated the evaluation questions, whether they addressed these questions through the report, the appropriateness of the evaluation design to the evaluation questions, etc. Both the factors included in the scoring system and their relative weights were established through a process that involved evaluation users, AID evaluation staff and outside experts on evaluation. The technique allows us to score reports on a 0–100 scale. In our pre-test the average score was 50, which is a good place for the mean if the idea of the technique is to help us improve and assess whatever we do. From a diagnostic perspective, we will be particularly interested in evaluations that score over 75 or under 25 as we review the data on the FY82 evaluations which we have now nearly finished scoring. By early next fiscal year, we intend to transmit to our evaluation staff the criteria we are using in these 'Academy Awards' as well as the pattern of scores we find with our first full analysis.

To supplement this approach to assessing evaluation quality we intend, as noted above, to begin asking our Missions to comment about the quality and utility of the evaluations they commission. We have also recently undertaken a study of opportunities for improving the utilisation of our evaluation work which is producing a range of other suggestions for assessing quality in terms of utilisation as opposed to technical quality which is covered by the 'meta-evaluation' technique discussed above. Among the experimental work we are already doing in this area is an effort to follow-up on a sample of past evaluations to determine whether the actions identified on the face sheets for evaluation reports have actually been implemented in the projects where the need for these actions was identified. While our work in this area is quite preliminary, we would expect to be in a position similar to our position with respect to understanding the quality aspects of evaluation within the next few years.

Storage, Retrieval, Secondary Analysis and Synthesis of Evaluation Work

As the preceding sections have suggested, until this year our storage and retrieval work was being carried out by the Development Information Utilisation Service which has for a number of years been located in our Science and Technology Bureau. The tasks of secondary analysis and synthesis, have been low level activities, with some responsibility lying in the Office of Development Information and some in the central Office of Evaluation in the Bureau for Program and Policy Coordination (PPC). Because these various functions are so critical to full utilisation of AID evaluation findings and lessons, and partly in response to a report on our utilisation of evaluation evidence prepared in June 1982 by the US General Accounting Office, AID transferred the Development Information and Utilisation Service into PPC this year and is now taking steps to bring the work of these units closer together and to devote additional attention to the secondary analysis and synthesis work required to provide evaluative information to potential users in a timely and useful fashion, particularly with respect to uses beyond the projects for which evaluations have been conducted. Changes in abstracting procedures for evaluations, programming of our computerised data bases to produce statistical as well as narrative reports on our evaluation holdings, our retrospective analysis of evaluation coverage, our experiments with 'meta-analysis' and other synthesis techniques and our current work on approaches for making evaluation information more readily usable in terms of user descriptions of what they are seeking all address recognised needs in this aspect of AID's overall evaluation work. The problems we are now addressing are in many ways side effects of our own success—they are problems that arise only after an evaluation system has been in operation for quite some time and questions of scale and amassed knowledge management become crucial to the further development and application of the system.

The Use of Evaluation Findings and Lessons

As indicated in the preceding sections, the primary responsibility for using evaluation findings and lessons lies with the AID staff responsible for designing and implementing foreign assistance activities. Evaluation staff play a supporting role in this process, but cannot play the lead role, by definition. Since the issue of utilisation has been a continuous theme throughout this paper, its treatment here is limited. As already noted, we are currently taking additional steps to ensure compliance with existing requirements that call for the use of evaluation findings and lessons in project and programme design. We are also calling for the use of evaluation findings and lessons in our country development strategy statements—our 'five-year' plans for work in a particular developing country. This spring we are also incorporating the requirement to employ evaluation findings and lessons in our annual budget submissions and for the past year we have been working closely with AID's policy development staff to ensure that our new series of policy papers benefited from AID's accumulated knowledge on topics covered by that series. In two areas where policy papers were being developed, we supplemented our normal workload with field studies of past experience as an additional input to the policy development process. We expect to continue this type of support for policy development work in the future, and, as suggested earlier we have written plans for evaluating the performance of AID at the country level. When implemented, these plans will provide another reasonably direct link to users and their forward planning needs.

New Directions in Evaluation Studies in AID

Several of the new directions AID evaluations are taking have already been identified and several others warrant identification. Listed below are some of the types of evaluation work which we currently anticipate will receive additional attention during the next few years:

a Country Programme Evaluations, designed to assess the overall effects of a programme of assistance to particular countries. We have some old experience with this idea as well as some new ideas. We also have better statements of the objectives of our country programmes which, over time, will serve as the basis for this work

b Tighter comparative evaluations of the effectiveness and impact of similar projects in different settings. To some degree this will emerge from our bureau level work, particularly for centrally managed programmes that have common objectives for all of their field operations

c Comparative evaluations that focus on the relative effectiveness of alternative approaches for achieving the same objective. Our current Africa Bureau evaluation of renewable energy systems is 'breaking ground' in this area by attempting to assess the relative effectiveness of wind, solar and other renewable energy systems for specific end-uses such as water pumping. The principles applied here are potentially extendable to examining, for example, the relative effectiveness of changing the types of food available in rural markets versus nutrition education for improving the quality of rural diets. While we expect to face great difficulties as we move in this direction, we see value in trying to overcome the obvious problems we will face

d Evaluations which focus on cross-cutting issues such as recurrent costs, types of implementation approaches, etc. We have already responded to the need for one such evaluation with a synthesis of what we knew from evaluation work about factors which affect the speed of project implementation. We can already foresee the need for other such management-oriented evaluations in areas that cut across traditional evaluation categories and topics.

Assistance to Developing Countries in Improving Their Evaluation Work

AID uses two basic approaches for assisting the developing countries to strengthen their evaluation capacity and their use of evaluation findings and lessons in their own forward planning. The first approach is through involving developing country personnel in the evaluations we initiate or which we build into our loan agreements. We believe that a positive attitude toward evaluation is best developed through participation. Only after people have a positive attitude toward evaluation and the use of evaluation findings and lessons do we find that their interest in techniques and systems rises dramatically. In our evaluation guidance we call for developing country participation in all of our field evaluations of on-going projects and programmes, for this type of evaluation provides the greatest opportunity to experience the full evaluative cycle: planning through the application of evaluation findings to forward action. One of the more complete examples of this work is in our Senegal

Mission, where the entire programme was jointly reviewed and evaluated by AID and the government as a basis for planning the future evolution of the programme.

Our second basic mechanism for supporting the work of the developing countries in evaluation is through direct assistance in the development of their evaluation capacity. This work subsumes the training we provide and arrange for in evaluation as well as our work in countries such as Nigeria and Thailand in helping the local government set up and administer evaluation units and evaluation-cum-monitoring systems for complex programmes.

As we assist developing countries improve their evaluation capacity and as we watch other bilateral and multilateral donors engage in similar work we are aware of a problem which may be emerging for the developing countries. This problem, which we casually refer to as the 'rabbits' problem, is worth some attention from the donor community. Over the past ten years, quite a few donor organisations have adopted evaluation systems which are roughly similar. In the sense that they apply common theoretical constructs they spring from a single 'rabbit', but like 'rabbits' they all differ slightly. As these donors assist the developing countries in installing evaluation systems, they are spawning still another generation of 'rabbits'—which by now look quite different from their second cousins, at least with respect to their terminology. The 'rabbits' problem is not a problem from the donor perspective—rather it occurs when different ministries in a single country install evaluation systems with support from different donors and after the fact find, to their dismay, that their evaluation systems cannot communicate with each other, thus posing a significant problem for the Ministry of Finance or whatever ministry has the lead role in overseeing planning and performance in all the other ministries in the country. This central ministry will either have to learn the languages of all of the second generation 'rabbits' it owns or, at some considerable cost, force its various 'rabbits' to start speaking a common evaluation language.

C3

The Indian Evaluation System
by Dr S. M. Shah, Adviser (Evaluation), Planning Commission, New Delhi

Evaluation is gradually emerging as an important function in public policy. With the emergence of planning in several countries, the need for evaluation of plan projects and programmes attained considerable importance. It is now well recognised that evaluation provides to the planners and policy makers important and timely feedback enabling a watch to be kept on progress being made in the execution of the schemes. This helps improve implementation, enhances the effectiveness of the programmes and even enables the reorientation of public policy and programmes in order to attain the desired or stated objectives. That evaluation can be a powerful tool to improve public policy has been amply demonstrated by the experience of evaluation work in India.

The Development of Evaluation Work

After India attained Independence in 1947, she launched the programmes of economic development in a planned and organised manner. The first Five-Year Plan (1951–6) was launched in the perspective of long-term development to attain growth with social justice. Initially, the Programme Evaluation Organisation (PEO) was established to evaluate the working of the 'Community Development Programme' in rural transformation covering more than 5000 community development blocks of population size approximately 100 000 each. The task before the PEO was to appraise the progress being made in carrying out the programme, evaluate and point out those methods proving successful and those which were not; also to assess the impact of the programme on the lives and economy of the people and generally to suggest directions in which new rural institutions could be built or refashioned. The PEO presented 'Annual Evaluation Reports' to the annual Conferences of Development Commissioners in charge of the programme on the working of the community development programme in the country.

Gradually, with the change in emphasis, the Community Development Programme itself moved towards new directions of Panchayati Raj institutions of decentralised development at village, Samiti, and Block Levels. In the last two Five-Year Plans, 1975–9 and 1980–5, emphasis has been laid on integrated rural development and on several other special programmes to ameliorate the conditions of the weaker sections of the society.

In consonance with the changes brought about in the structure of the programmes, the evaluation organisation itself was called upon to shoulder newer responsibilities and the enlarging of its field of activities. This it did in good measure. Evaluation studies now touch all sectors—agriculture, irrigation, rural electrification, small industry, health, nutrition, education, panchayati raj institutions, co-operatives, etc.

Besides the Central PEO, every state in India has a State Evaluation Organisation (SEO) to evaluate the programmes under the State sector. Five-Year Plans in India are implemented through the machinery of the State Governments, although there are certain central sector projects implemented through the Central Government. Hence the need arose for each State Government to have a State Level Evaluation Organisation. Since 1966, the Central PEO assiduously nurtured the growth of State evaluation organisations as equal partners.

The PEO, with its headquarters within the Planning Commission, New Delhi, evaluates through its 34 field offices the working of various schemes launched in the Five-Year Plans. In addition, every state (now 22) has its own SEO. Together with the Centre and the States, India has at present a corpus of 870 professional evaluators, well versed in survey research methods, and evaluation techniques. India today has the largest evaluation organisation in the world, including both developed and developing countries.

Structure and Functions

The PEO is established within the Planning Commission, with its headquarters in New Delhi. The PEO is a three-tier organisation. At the headquarters which forms the apex, the PEO has 12 Deputy Advisers belonging to different disciplines—agricultural economics, institutional economics, sociology, cultural anthropology and social work, statistics, research methodology and technical co-ordination, besides a Deputy Secretary in charge of administration and personnel management. There is also a Director in charge of computer services division with two dozen programmers, senior programmers and punching staff. These officers assist the Adviser (Evaluation) in charge of PEO whose status is sufficiently high as that of Additional Secretary to the Government of India. This group mainly selects the subjects for evaluation, designs new evaluation studies, organises and oversees the field investigations, prepares tabulation plans and analyses of data, and prepares draft reports which are finalised by the Adviser (Evaluation). It controls and directs the field operations and trains the field staff by organising training seminars for pre-testing of the designs and schedules. The Adviser (Evaluation) confers with the counterparts in Central Ministries and acts as the main spokesman for the Planning Commission in all matters concerning the findings of evaluation studies. He also helps the Planning Commission in bringing to its notice the strong and weak points of the programmes being evaluated, and assists the Planning Commission in the formulation of future plans and even in the restructuring of certain programmes on the basis of the feedback he receives from the field.

For its day-to-day working, the PEO is under the Deputy Chairman/Minister for Planning to the Government of India. The Prime Minister is the Chairman of the Planning Commission. The PEO reports directly to the Deputy Chairman of the Planning Commission and is answerable only to the Planning Commission, not to any administrative ministry. PEO thus has complete technical independence to express its findings without any fear. Hence, its reports are faithful and truthful, based on data or information collected by its own field staff. In reporting, the PEO puts most emphasis on data generated by its own staff through primary collection, rather than relying on secondary data.

The middle tier of the PEO consists of seven Regional Evaluation Officers (REO) located in different regions, with their headquarters at Bombay, Madras, Hyderabad, Lucknow, Calcutta, Chandigarh and Jaipur. They oversee and supervise and assist a group of four to six Project Evaluation Officers spread out in every State (one in each or two if the State is large, eg Uttar Pradesh, Maharastra, etc). The REOs are assisted in administrative matters by a Superintendent and in technical matters by a Research Officer/Assistant Director with a back-up of four senior and junior level investigators. The REOs carry out the field studies allotted by the headquarters, New Delhi Office, deploy the staff, undertake five to ten per cent on-the-spot scrutiny of schedules being canvassed, assemble the filled-in schedules, and scrutinise them before submitting them to headquarters for further processing. Often, meetings of REOs are held to discuss the new studies and transmit other important instructions. REO meetings are also utilised to discuss draft reports.

The REOs keep a rapport with the State capitals and collect data on State level schedules incorporating guidelines and progress of various schemes. They assist the Adviser (Evaluation) and his deputy advisers in on-the-spot evaluation field visits, and bring to his notice urgent studies required for evaluation in the States under their beat. Thus the REO is an important link between headquarters and the field units.

The bottom tier of the PEO consists of its 34 field offices dotted around different states and manned by Project Evaluation Officers assisted by two field investigators each. They are principally responsible for collecting data from district and block levels and supervise, assist and scrutinise the work of field investigators. The beneficiary/non-beneficiary households form the respondents from whom data are collected through interview methods.

State Evaluation Organisations

The structure of the SEO differs from State to State. Certain populous states like Maharastra, Gujarat, Karnataka, Rajasthan, Madhya Pradesh, Uttar Pradesh, West Bengal, Bihar, Orissa, have more than 50 evaluation officers each, whereas some others have comparatively much smaller staff. Evaluation organisation in the North Eastern States is as yet still in the offing.

Most State evaluation organisations are headed by a Director assisted by Deputy and Assistant Directors. The SEO works under the State Planning Department/Board, though a few are yet under Department of Finance or General Administration. The SEOs submit their reports to the Secretary, Planning. The reports are discussed by State evaluation committees comprising of heads of different departments and headed by State Chief Secretaries and in some cases by Chief Ministers. Action on the reports is taken by Administrative Departments.

In dissemination of reports, there are differences between the Central and the State evaluation organisation. Almost all reports of the Central PEO are issued and published for wider distribution to the government and the public. As soon as the Adviser (Evaluation) has prepared the report and the Deputy Chairman has approved its release, the accredited officer of the Press Information Bureau, Government of India prepares a press handout and releases important findings. This is picked up by radio, television and daily newspapers and receives good media coverage. These reports draw the attention of the Parliament and its various Committees, eg Estimates Committees, Consultative Committees and in particular the Public Accounts Committee. This public pressure compels the administrative department(s) whose programmes are being evaluated to take early remedial measures to improve performance.

The PEO has reported on (1) Employment Guarantee Scheme (1978), (2) Food-For-Work Programme (1979), (3) Rural Water Supply (1981) and (4) Integrated Child Development Services Programme (1982) which drew in particular both national and international attention.

The SEO's reports are by and large not available in published or printed form. Lately, at the behest of the Central PEO, some States have brought out findings of evaluation studies carried out in the past ten years in a summary form on the occasion of Regional Workshops on Evaluation hosted by them.

Compared to the Central PEO, the SEO has been able to cover a much larger sample on account of more staff being available to it. Joint evaluation between the Centre and the States has thus been to great mutual advantage.

Main Strength and Weaknesses

The PEO has been able to fulfil the expectation of being the 'Eyes and Ears' of the Planning Commission. As a result of its evaluations several programmes have been restructured. Since its recommendations are action-oriented it has been possible to take immediate follow-up action. As a matter of fact, at the time the evaluation reports are published, a 'Note' is added from the Ministry whose programme is evaluated indicating action taken in improvements based on the evaluation findings.

However important the PEO's work has been, it must be admitted that in terms of plan outlay, the schemes examined by the PEO form only a small portion of the total outlay. Its main work has been in evaluating schemes of beneficiary-oriented programmes amenable to survey research. Apart from 'before' and 'after' and 'treatment' and 'control', the PEO has not been able to carry out benefit–cost analyses which require much larger samples and more detailed data.

The PEO has been able to select from each State one district, two blocks, four villages and 40 households, giving altogether around 3000 to 4000 households as sample size. Undoubtedly, the sample size is meagre, and it has to be buttressed with qualitative data. PEO staff being limited in size it has not been found possible to enlarge the sample. Also, the available staff at headquarters for processing and analysis of data needs to be strengthened. There is a need to have a fully-fledged training division, documentation division and a technical co-ordination division to discharge the organisational functions more effectively.

The expanding horizons of evaluation call for greater responsibility to be shouldered by the PEO; and if the PEO were to undertake a larger number of studies, its number of field investigators would need to be increased fourfold. Presently, the PEO field units (including regional evaluation units) have no vehicle of their own. This needs to be provided to facilitate the coverage and speed of their field work.

The status of REOs needs to be upgraded to that of Joint Director to effectively interface with State evaluation directors.

Because of the dynamic process of economic development, evaluation personnel need continuous training in methods and techniques. During the last three years 1979–82, the PEO has organised about 12 regional workshops and training programmes and imparted training to 228 Senior, 124 Supervisory (Middle Level) and 27 Junior Evaluation Personnel both at the Centre and in the States. More rigorous efforts are required by the States to upgrade the skills of their Junior Level Evaluation Personnel.

Evaluation System under UN and Other Donor Agencies

India is happy that the UN and several donor agencies like the World Bank, the United States Agency for International Development (USAID), and the Asian Development Bank (ADB) are paying increasing attention to the evaluation of the programmes being assisted by them. The Inter-Agency Meeting on Evaluation held at Geneva on 29 March 1982 was a high-water mark signifying the importance of evaluation in all the UN Agencies. The UN Joint Inspection Unit (JIU) should hold such meetings annually, and review and assist evaluation work being developed throughout the world.

International agencies should hold similar regional workshops on evaluation, discussing the findings of evaluation studies undertaken in the respective regions and giving a thrust to evaluation work. They can also assist independent research institutions to take a lead and organise regional meetings, seminars and workshops on evaluation methods and techniques.

In the field of training, the United Nations Educational, Scientific and Cultural Organisation (UNESCO) which has brought out some very important material in this respect, should spearhead the activity and locate institutions to fund training programmes and bring out fresh material on evaluation. For example, in view of the large number of evaluation studies being carried by USAID, and at the PEO, New Delhi, a 'Synthesis' should be commissioned in order to bring out the main approaches being developed and the utility (or impact) of evaluation work on public policy. Similarly, such documentation can be prepared, in case studies, for other countries and other agencies.

As in the field of improving public policy in a country (such as India) evaluation can also help improve public policy at the international level as well. Programmes under the United Nations Children's Fund (UNICEF), the Food and Agricultural Organisation of the UN (FAO), the International Fund for Agricultural Development (IFAD), and the United Nations Fund for Population Activities (UNFPA) can be evaluated across countries in order to bring out successes or failures and the impact of these programmes. This is a field in which national evaluation authorities can contribute a lot in co-operation with international donor agencies.

There is an urgent need, because of international concern, to evaluate the various food-for-work type programmes under the World Food Programme (WFP) and their effectiveness in different countries. Similarly the special employment programmes assisted by the International Labour Organisation (ILO), and above all the health and nutrition programmes being assisted by UNICEF. More case studies need to be carried out cross-country and cross-programmes so that future directions for the development of these programmes are clear, and are based on rational grounds. UNICEF, WFP, ILO and UNESCO need to have strong Evaluation Secretariats at their headquarters.

UNESCO could initiate, sponsor and organise a World Congress on Evaluation bringing together both professionals and practitioners on a common platform. Such a Congress would ignite evaluation work in several countries and focus attention on urgent issues. It would help build up the evaluation climate and receptivity in recipient countries.

Bilateral Donors

Whereas international agencies worldwide can create interest and demand for programmes to be evaluated in various fields, bilateral donors can effectively develop 'Joint Evaluation' studies under common aegis to review the implementation of programmes, measure their impact and decide on future development. Whereas international donors (like the World Bank) are distant, bilateral donors are nearer. They should jointly carry out or assign studies, and benefit from their results. They should also hold joint workshops.

No aid can be complete until an evaluation report has been submitted on it. Bilateral donors could assign this task on a consultancy basis to social scientists of proven ability in the host country. Aid agencies should be obliged to take ameliorative action on the reports so submitted. To the bilateral donor, these evaluations should help them in choosing activities that are effective and in rejecting those that are not properly carried out. Evaluation work can remove some of the misunderstandings and irritants between donors and recipients by providing a common rationale for aid assessment, and by confirming international relations as a whole it can help to build a strong co-operative 'commonwealth'.

One easy and practical way forward for bilateral donors would be for them to arrange exchange visits and to sponsor fellowships for joint activities in evaluation research. This would help to upgrade skills. Several courses, for example, of three to six months' duration, are already being organised under the Colombo Plan. The Government could assign specific courses to selected institutions, help to build up the faculty and so develop evaluation expertise under Colombo Plan auspices.

The Economic Development Institute (EDI) of the World Bank should have responsibility (like UNESCO) for the development of pure research in evaluation work, with emphasis on the methods and techniques in the field of evaluation. EDI could institute fellowships, and organise one or two months' 'appreciation courses' for top policy makers and practitioners so that they are able to recognise and value evaluation research. Evaluation has expanding horizons, and the future is full of promising developments.

PART

QUO VADIS?

A Visionary Look at where Evaluation is Heading in the Years Ahead

by Mr R. J. Berg, Overseas Development Council, Washington, USA

(Mr Berg was chairman of the Evaluation Group of the Development Assistance Committee (DAC) of the Organisation for Economic Cooperation and Development (OECD) and directed the evaluation work of the United States Agency for International Development (USAID). Because of his important contributions to the development of evaluation work in the USA and internationally, he was invited to contribute this special forward-looking paper at the end of the Conference. His statements are his personal views.)

It is a high honour to speak at the end of this Conference, before this distinguished sponsorship and audience, in an Institute where many famous discussions of development have taken place. Having heard a discussion of the current standing of the field of evaluation of development, it is perhaps useful to reflect on the possibilities of the longer future, and on what we might wish for this now-worldwide movement to improve the quality of development.

Many at this Conference are representatives of donors and citizens of donor governments. A traditional interest has been that the micro-evidence of the effectiveness of the projects and programmes supported by the donors be solidly based. Nothing which I say should be interpreted as wanting to detract from the essential need of donors to be accountable to themselves and their publics for the efficacy of what they finance.

But, as has perhaps too infrequently been said, evaluation of development is primarily a mechanism to be accountable to the people we are trying to help. It is they who stand to gain or lose most. So, I welcome the view of the World Bank's Director General, Operations Evaluation, in his paper, that ten years hence donors ought to be primarily dependent upon developing countries to supply their evaluations.* I would contend that the closer the point responsible for evaluation lies to the actual programme being evaluated, the easier it should be to improve the socio-economic performance of the programme on the basis of the evaluations, and thus the more effective the evaluation process should be so far as the intended beneficiaries are concerned.

Do we need to wait another ten years to make the switch? Surely not! Some developing countries can take over the responsibility for evaluating their donor-assisted programmes sooner than others. It will be interesting to see which donors take the risk; who will start the process of placing the full responsibility for evaluation on selected developing countries sooner rather than later?

Many of us remember our surprise, as the Chinese started their aid programmes, when they sent teams around the countries of the proposed recipients to search out and help develop local sources of supply. I think the International Fund for Agricultural Development (IFAD) is consciously emulating the Chinese as IFAD plans the monitoring and evaluation of the agricultural projects they support by first surveying local capabilities to

---

*Mr Weiner's judgement is that 'If present trends continue, ten years from now the Bank's project performance assessments could be based predominantly on evaluations by borrowers rather than on evaluations by Bank staff as at present.' Since Bank projects are larger and often far more complex than those of other donors, I take the liberty of extending the judgement to the wider field of donors.

monitor and evaluate. Sometimes units exist that are able to take on the tasks, but sometimes units will need to be created or assisted as part of the aid package. More of us could take this approach of using and building upon local public administration to assess the quality of local development.

But the switch from donors to recipients will likely involve only responsibility for micro project-based evaluations. There will remain a requirement for donor evaluation units to respond to the need for higher levels of synthesis and analysis, levels of concern which our profession is now approaching with undue caution.

Evaluation, like all key management systems, has an important role in modifying organisational behaviour. While donor evaluators have been useful in pointing out successes and failures at the local level, and thus leading donor institutions to ever more careful (and lengthy!) project design and sectoral guidelines, donor evaluators have been less successful in focusing attention on the bigger issues. It is good, however, that some donors are beginning to focus more on the sectoral patterns of findings drawn from their own evaluation experience.

Yet key political and development questions are still not being addressed by multilateral and bilateral donors, and perhaps we need to expand the intellectual horizons of the field a bit more.

In the widest perspective one must start at the global level. Here I address our United Nations colleagues and our governments, all of which are vote-holders in the UN system.

The UN is not yet equipped to answer fundamental concerns about its development performance. Such concerns include: Is the UN emphasis on Development Decades, the 'year of the' this and that, and global conferences on specific development topics, the most productive use of UN resources to promote development issues? Is the UN's allocation of its financial and human resources for development programmes germane, or optimal? Based on its performance, where has the UN system been at its best? Where are improvements most needed? How can these improvements best be brought about? The UN has a scattering of the infrastructure needed to answer these questions, but its resources are currently devoted to lesser questions.

I would ask similar questions of the Group of 77 and the OECD. Both groups are important yet, to this observer, both could stand major improvement and neither has even the beginnings of a professional capacity for introspection about evaluative questions of performance.

In addition, the functioning of the interaction of the Group of 77 (which represents the developing countries), and Group B (representing the OECD countries) must improve across the board.* The well-known failures of the North-South negotiations tend to obscure real progress on some issues. But since neither the failures nor the successes have been evaluated by the responsible negotiating parties, the lessons from these experiences, which might shape future more productive negotiations, are yet to be learned.

A future agenda for developing country evaluators is difficult to suggest

*One, perhaps parochial, manifestation of the lack of co-operation between the G–77 and Group B countries is seen in the current consideration of the UNDP's proposal to upgrade significantly their evaluation activities. Friction and suspicion between the two blocks are obscuring the more fundamental shared concerns of both over the need to improve the functioning of the multilateral system.

since so little research work has yet been done (and even less published) on the public administration conditions and problems of national and other evaluation units in these countries, and no work exists that I know of which systematically assesses the quality of their products. But on the basis of a fairly large number of discussions in developing countries, I make a few suggestions.

First, I would note that the range of competencies is rather wider in developing countries than among the donors. While a larger proportion of donors have evaluation programmes than developing countries, I find the sophistication of some evaluations carried out by developing countries to be greater than the donors', whilst some meet many fewer of the tests of evaluation. Thus it is harder to make general statements about the state of evaluation in developing countries than it is to make such statements about donor evaluations.

In many developing countries the evaluation function is fragile. Obviously it is a more political act to make a critique of a local project than it is (for the donors) to make a critique of a foreign project or programme. Hence the risks to developing country evaluators are greater and the need to offer them institutional protection is correspondingly greater. (This is certainly not to say that attempts to politically influence donor evaluation units are unknown.) In fostering evaluation entities in developing countries donors and local authorities will need to learn to both take, and provide for the taking of, risks (though allowing appropriate freedom to make findings and recommendations) and to help create the institutional environment necessary to permit the function to operate.

In some governments there is the question of where to locate the function. A range of experience exists for both smaller and larger governments to observe. Units which evaluate are found attached to the office of the head of state, in planning ministries and in line ministries (or a combination). In some larger countries the evaluation function is also represented at the provincial level.

For many developing countries, then, there are important public administration choices to be made for establishing and operating evaluation programmes. While it will be tempting to model new evaluation units after donor experience, there is sufficient experience in the developing countries in both monitoring and evaluation entities to find perhaps more applicable models there. Obviously, there are substantive evaluation questions in plentiful supply for developing countries. I shall not attempt an agenda of these, in part since I have seen but a small fraction of the evaluation output of the evaluations done by developing countries and in part since some of what follows applies to those countries as well.

At the donor level, some of the most basic policy concerns have not yet been adequately addressed. I shall name but three.

Fundamentally, the totality of donor evaluations results should be assessed to attempt to answer from very large sets of data whether development assistance works. We are closer to being able to address this issue effectively than ever before in the relatively short history of evaluation. Important holdings of project and sectoral performance information are being accumulated by a number of evaluation authorities. If this information is properly analysed, donors should be able to establish norms for effectiveness impact to be able to compare donor, sectoral and country performance

Donors will need to do far more cross analysis of the information collected on project and sectoral performance. An early priority should be to review the experience of helping particularly disadvantaged groups within poor societies. There is some data for this kind of analysis, but it is scattered. Over time, donors will need to assure that more systematic data is included on key issues, often social in nature, which are neglected now

But we have very little data on a third question, which, in my view, is the most serious problem affecting donor effectiveness. That is the question of aid co-ordination. This is not the place to note the scandals and the high costs of so many unlinked official and private doers of good. Suffice it to say that we must jump at any decent case of co-ordination for prompt evaluation.*

Evaluators must also learn to co-ordinate better. Donors will increasingly need to subordinate their evaluation agendas to the wishes of developing countries. Donors will need to carry out joint exercises. Donors will need to curtail frequent and unco-ordinated calls for national and sectoral data—in response to which some developing countries have felt called upon to create vast data collection entities. (In one case, a country noted for its co-operation with donors, the central government actually employs more enumerators per 100 000 population than they do agricultural extension agents or rural health workers.) And donors will need to resist stampeding into new problem areas, such as assisting the evaluation units of developing countries, lest we trample on the very organisations we want to help.

In many of these policy-urgent areas, donors will need to learn on the basis of a few number of cases, since only a few cases exist. We should not stand aside and wait for the experience to pile up in sufficient case numbers to make the analysis easy. We will have to be willing to risk analysis soon, or we will be judged to be irrelevant. And let us not be mistaken: the field of evaluation is enjoying very unusual times. We are being accepted and fostered whether we are relevant or not. We are one of the few occupations which thrives in times of economic depression when parliaments are desperate for information to justify programmes, particularly such traditionally controversial programmes as international assistance. We are a counter-cyclical phenomenon; how else can one explain the growth of the evaluation unit in Australia's aid agency from seven to 14 people at the very time when their overall employment level

---

*Indeed, there are so few enduring cases of productive co-ordination that donors also ought to finance pilot projects of co-ordination which, if proven useful through the usual tests of evaluation, could be initiated on a wider basis. I have in mind experimenting with such concepts as common in-country secretariats for private and voluntary organisations which would be *the* focal point for negotiating with officials, packaging 'wholesale' projects and administering counterpart contributions to the retail, ie, village level implementing organisations. Such experiments might not only save time in the capital city for government officials, but might also enable the retailing donor agencies to staff more on the basis of technical skills as opposed to the need to staff for capital city negotiating skills.

was shrinking from 500 to 350 people?* I am sure that the field of donor evaluation will need to prove its policy relevance if it is to maintain its current strength through the time when the economies of the North recover . . . should that occur!

Over time, as our shelves groan with good reports, will evaluators need to maintain comprehensive, standard formatted systems of evaluation? I would hope not. For developers are supposed to be managers of risk. Evaluators will be able to identify, through the literature the field has been producing, some types of development projects which can be carried out with a very high probability of success, for example, construction of rural roads in cases where new access is provided and where there are appreciable numbers of people. For such types of projects, project managers in developing countries can be guided to monitor very selected key factors influencing the outcomes of such projects and then donors and developing countries can risk *not* evaluating such projects as long as the monitoring data looks appropriate.

However, in programme areas of uncertainty, such as in many kinds of rural health services or programmes aimed at nomadic peoples, we may need to reduce the risks to governments and the people involved by more intensive monitoring and evaluation until these programmes can be launched with far more certainty of success. The operating principle, I suspect, will be to assume that less major evaluation is better until proven otherwise.

Donors must also develop relative standards of performance. Too many find too much comfort in holding to uniform standards applied on a global basis. To those who assume that a project with an internal economic rate of return of ten per cent or more is good, and below that is unacceptable, I would contend that a project with a rate of return of two per cent in today's Ghana may be a miracle of development, while we might wish to replace the fellow whose Singapore project only yields a rate of return of 15 per cent. As it is now, the Singapore man may well be given a promotion while the one responsible for the Ghana project will be shipped off to the motor pool.

This Conference on the Evaluation of Aid Projects and Programmes has provided a most useful opportunity to learn from others' experience. It has been valuable and the ODA is to be commended for the idea and management of the occasion.

As I have indicated, I see the evaluation of development activities becoming more policy oriented, more tactical in the use of our limited evaluation resources and more dependent upon developing countries.

The value of sharing experience and providing useful peer pressure is available to us as donors since we can afford it. This opportunity is not available to the evaluation authorities of the South since they cannot afford such meetings. Some of us have long felt the need for a professional association of national evaluation leaders, but clearly the organising costs and the participation of the South would need to be subsidised. Donor organisations would be acting with considerable foresight if they would help foster peer linkages of the evaluators in the South who one day will be responsible for the quality review of governmental programmes aimed at three-quarters of the world. And, if this peer group included the minority

*As reported by the Australian Development Assistance Bureau in a 1981 DAC survey of member evaluation units.

world of the North, I would expect the donor countries to benefit considerably . . . perhaps even to the extent where the national governments of the North became as sophisticated in the evaluation of their domestic programmes as they are in the evaluation of their foreign endeavours.

Discussion

Ms M. Hageboeck, (Division Chief, Programme Evaluation, United States Agency for International Development (USAID)) commented that 'ex-post' to the aid donor meant when the donor's own role had been completed, but usually that was the point when the project was just coming into operation, ie if the donor did not evaluate at a later stage he might miss many valuable lessons relating to the operation and maintenance of projects or concerning the eventual outworking of aid projects that had been innovative or experimental in character. She thought that evaluators in aid agencies were going to have to tackle this problem in the near future.

Mr R. J. Berg (Overseas Development Council, Washington) agreed that it would make better developmental sense if donors could foster review and evaluation systems that covered not merely their specific provision of inputs that might represent only ten per cent of the total but also the remaining 90 per cent as well. Of course this might in time involve a changing political relationship, ie as the recipient country's economy develops the relationship could change from one of aid assistance to trade investment. Enhancing the recipient's capability in such fields as budgeting monitoring and evaluation, made good sense in preparation for a more mature partnership in the future. However, a very real problem was the competition on the part of the donors for the time of a small number of key officials in the developing countries—often they were putting in say only ten per cent of the development budget of the country but were demanding 90 per cent of the time of the key officials. The problem was increasing with the growing number of donor agencies. At present there were about 34 bilateral aid agencies and 60 multilateral agencies. In addition the Development Assistance Committee (DAC) had listed 745 voluntary aid institutions. The typical United Nations Development Programme (UNDP) list for a country included about 100 sources of aid. Soon the middle-income countries would be starting up their own aid agencies and the problems would get even worse. He thought some drastic solutions would have to be sought, such as some sort of 'wholesaling' mechanism to help match aid agencies to potential projects; this might cause problems to countries wanting to have their aid contributions recognised by the world at large but a little ingenuity should lead to ways round that problem.

Mr J. White (Organisation for Economic Cooperation and Development (OECD), Paris) commented that the way ahead as chartered by Mr Berg seemed at first sight to offer an exciting alternative to the usual level of discussion on evaluation, which generally focused on marginal changes at the edges that might bring the recipients a bit more into the picture, together with analysing realised rates of return and so on. But in fact it did not because it was exclusively about the narrow field of evaluation and did not tackle the wider aid issues.

On the question of co-ordination he said it was untrue that there was no data on how the existing measures of co-ordination were functioning. The Organisation of Petroleum Exporting Countries (OPEC) donors now had regular meetings at technical level and there were various co-ordinating sub-groups within the DAC (eg regular meetings were held of the Nordic donors and on follow-up to the conference on the Least Developed Countries, also on how to strengthen the role of the UNDP resident co-ordinators).

As to the value of the growing amount of evaluation work now being done by donors, he suggested that it was not enough just to look for marginal improvements as a result of this work (eg of the sort listed in the ODA's booklet 'The Lessons of Experience'). He thought that evaluation departments should have a role, working in unison with others engaged in aid planning and programming, in improving the quality of aid operations on a broader front. He thought that that was really the key issue that evaluators should be addressing.

PART

CONCLUSIONS AND FOLLOW-UP ACTION

E1

Closing Address by Mr R. S. Porter, Deputy Secretary and Chief Economist, ODA

In his speech winding up the Conference, Mr Porter said that some participants had asked him exactly why the ODA had taken the rather unusual step of holding the Conference—was there perhaps some ulterior motive? The answer was that ODA had no ulterior motive in mind and its sole objective had been to share with a wider group of interested people the experience that ODA had gained in what was a fairly new field. It was in ODA's mind that such people as evaluators, consultants, academics, and representatives of developing countries, might all have an important contribution to make to the development of the subject. The ODA was well aware that some of the institutions represented had been working in the evaluation field longer than ODA and had devoted considerably more resources to it. ODA had indeed learnt a lot and the Conference had proved very worthwhile.

Mr Porter listed four main topics that had struck him as particularly important and on which ODA would want to go away and reflect very carefully to see how it could improve its performance in these fields. They were as follows:

a *The Relationship between Monitoring and Evaluation*
Mr Porter felt that ODA would need to reconsider its compartmentalised approach, if for no other reason than that one clearly had to rely to a considerable extent on the information generated during the monitoring process as a basis for evaluation. If proper machinery were not set up for achieving this a lot of effort would be wasted. One of the problems would be that a lot of the data would be scattered among different ODA files and something would need to be done in that area

b *Role of the Developing Countries*
He said he had been particularly impressed by the discussion on this topic. After all the scene of the action was there in the developing countries, and in one sense the evaluations were being done largely for their benefit. But all too often their direct involvement in the exercise was small. He well understood the reasons for this, but suggested that a distinction should be made between formal and informal involvement. The developing countries, for good reasons, might not feel it appropriate to attach representatives to donor-sponsored evaluation teams, but that need not prevent the team from having full and frank interchanges with the host country. Indeed he could not see how one could carry out a sensible evaluation without this being the case. It boiled down to a question of how desirable it was for there to be more formal involvement on the part of the host countries. He also pointed out that a lot of evaluation studies carried out by donors were related primarily to the donor's own aid procedures and it would not be appropriate for the developing countries to have a formal involvement in

these. They also raised difficult questions of the confidentiality of the reports since there did not seem to be any particular reason why the donor should display his wares to the critical scrutiny of the rest of the world. He felt that the all-important thing was for the donor to learn the lessons and see that they are incorporated in future aid activities.

Nevertheless, having said that he agreed that there needed to be more involvement in the evaluation process by developing countries and the ODA would give this more serious thought

c *Scope of Evaluations*
Mr Porter referred to Mr J. White's pleas for evaluators to tackle the broad issues of aid policy and not be content merely with 'fringe' improvements. He thought evaluators would be better advised to generally eschew these broad policy or strategy issues and to concentrate on issues of aid management. Of course in the process of carrying out the evaluations wider issues would inevitably be raised, and evaluations had a role to play in focusing attention on these issues which in turn might be investigated at greater depth by research institutes or by other appropriate agencies. Evaluation studies had often touched on these issues but he thought they were better tackled by means of special research studies financed for example from the Social Science Research Programme. The ODA Evaluation Department could not cope with such issues unless it were to be given very much bigger resources

d *The Role of ODA's Project Appraisal Guide*
There had been a number of comments regarding the implications of evaluation findings for ODA's Project Appraisal Guide (which he emphasised was a 'guide' and not a didactic manual) and he agreed that after six years it was time to review it in the light of the findings of evaluation work, particularly for instance the usefulness of such appraisal techniques as elaborate exercises in shadow pricing.

In conclusion Mr Porter said that the Conference had scored several 'firsts'. It was the first set-piece conference that ODA had organised for many years (probably since the Cambridge Conferences of the 1960s). It was also the first, certainly on such a scale, to be held at the Institute of Development Studies; and it was the first Conference ODA had held on the subject of evaluation. It was hoped to prepare a report on the proceedings which might in due course turn itself into a book.

Finally Mr Porter closed the Conference by expressing thanks to Professor M. Faber for making available the splendid facilities of the Institute; to his staff particularly Mrs N. Tattersall and Mrs J. McCabe for their valuable assistance; to Dr Cracknell who had first suggested the holding of the Conference and had organised the programme; to Mr C. N. Britton and his assistants in the Evaluation Department for the support they had given throughout; and to the shorthand writer who had taken the verbatim report. Finally he thanked all those who had participated in the Conference, particularly the visitors from overseas, all of whom had helped to make it such a successful event.

APPENDICES

APPENDIX I
List of Principal Speakers and Contributors to Discussions

A Principal Speakers   *Page(s)*

Mr R. J. Berg	Senior Fellow, Overseas Development Council, Washington *5, 26, 27, 33, 35, 36, 43, 123, 129*
Mr R. A. Browning	Deputy Secretary, ODA *7, 27, 32, 39, 44*
Dr B. E. Cracknell	Head, Evaluation Department, ODA *2, 6, 11, 18, 21, 26, 27, 28, 33, 34, 36, 39*
Dr G. D. Gwyer	Natural Resources Economist, ODA *46, 59*
Ms M. Hageboeck	Office of Evaluation, USAID *35, 42, 102, 129*
Mr R. S. Porter	Deputy Secretary and Chief Economist, ODA *91, 132*
Dr S. M. Shah	Adviser (Evaluation), Planning Commission, New Delhi *36, 44, 117*
Mr J. N. Stevens	Economist, ODA *21, 41*
Mr A. P. Thomas	Assistant Director, Technical Co-operation Training Department, British Council *76, 82*
Mr B. P. Thomson	Economist, ODA *21, 83, 92*
Mr M. L. Weiner	Director-General, Operations Evaluation, IBRD *18, 43, 94*
Mrs J. M. White	Economist, Transport and Road Research Laboratory (now with ODA) *64, 73*
Mr J. K. Wright	Under Secretary, ODA *6, 12, 13, 19, 20, 26, 30, 31, 33, 34*

B Contributors to Discussions
Consultants

Mr W. Bor	Llewelyn-Davies Weeks *27, 73*
Mr J. Jacobs	Freelance *5, 11, 30, 39, 40, 42, 82*
Mr I. H. McLean	Mackay and Schnellman Ltd *34*
Mr J. D. Mettam	Bertlin & Partners *70*
Mr T. P. O'Sullivan	T. P. O'Sullivan & Partners *10, 72*

Overseas Organisations

Mr A. R. Ayazi	Food and Agriculture Organisation, Rome *17, 41, 57*
Mr J. Heidler	United Nations High Commission for Refugees, Geneva *36*
Mr F. G. Holder	World Food Programme, Rome *39, 41, 56, 71*
Mr J. Loup	French Ministry for Co-operation and Development *11*
Mr P. G. Rwelamira	African Development Bank *26, 30*

Mr G. Schwab	International Labour Organisation, Geneva *5, 32*
Mr J. White	Organisation for Economic Cooperation and Development, Paris *18, 27, 30, 80, 91, 129*
Mr K. Winkel	Danish International Development Agency *20, 34, 42*

Universities/Institutes

Dr I. Carruthers	Wye College *28, 43, 58*
Prof. D. Colman	University of Manchester *39, 57*
Mr A. Jennings	University of Leicester *91*
Mr T. Killick	Overseas Development Institute *90*
Dr R. M. Lawson	Humberside College of Higher Education *39, 59*
Dr M. Lipton	Institute of Development Studies *56, 71*
Mr D. McNeill	Development Planning Unit, London *19*
Mr S. Maxwell	Institute of Development Studies *34*
Mr L. P. Taylor	Selly Oak Colleges *35, 43*
Mr M. Whitby	University of Newcastle upon Tyne *80*
Mr P. J. Wood	University of Oxford *6, 58*

Associated Bodies/Scientific Units

Mr R. D. Bell	National Institute of Agricultural Engineering *58*
Mr D. Brewin	TETOC, British Council *26*
Mr D. R. Drabble	Commonwealth Development Corporation *12*
Mr J. L. Hine	Transport & Road Research Laboratory *72*

ODA Personnel

Mr W. A. Dodd	Chief Education Adviser *6*
Dr D. N. F. Hall	Principal Fisheries Adviser *19, 81*
Mr A. A. Kingshotte	Corps of Specialists *57, 72*

APPENDIX II
Complete List of Participants

Evaluation Departments Overseas

1   Mr A. R. Ayazi
    Chief, Evaluation Service

Food and Agricultural Organisation
of the United Nations (FAO)
Via Delle Terme di Caracalla
00100 Rome, Italy

2   Ms M. Balbanova
    Evaluation Co-ordinator

International Atomic Energy Agency
(IAEA)
Wagramerstrasse 5, P.O. Box 100
A-1400 Vienna, Austria

3   Mr R. J. Berg

Overseas Development Council
1717 Massachusetts Avenue NW 501
Washington DC 20036, USA

4   Ms M. Hageboeck

United States Agency for International
Development (USAID)
Washington DC 20523, USA

5   Mr C. Hancock
    USAID-Consultant

20 Washington Drive
Windsor, Berkshire, England SL4 4NS

6   Mr R. Harari
    Chief, Bureau of
    Programming and
    Management

International Labour Organisation
(ILO)
CH-1211 Geneva 22
Switzerland

7   Mr J. Heidler
    Chief, Policy Planning
    and Research Unit

United Nations High Commissioner
for Refugees (UNHCR)
Palais des Nations
CH-1211 Geneva 10
Switzerland

8   Mr S Higuchi
    Snr Assistant of Economic
    Co-operation, Economic
    Co-operation Bureau

Ministry of Foreign Affairs
Aid Policy Division
Kasumigaseki, Chiyodaku
Tokyo, Japan

9   Mr F. G. Holder
    Director, Evaluation
    Service

UN/FAO World Food Programme
Via Delle Terme di Caracalla
00100 Rome, Italy

10 Mr H. Ikonen
    Evaluation Officer

Ministry for Foreign Affairs
Dept for International Development
Co-operation (FINNIDA)
Mannerheimintie 15C
00260 Helsinki 26, Finland

11	Mr H. Kjekshus Head, Evaluation and Research	Norwegian Agency for International Development (NORAD) P.O. Box 8142 Oslo-Dep, Oslo 1, Norway
12	Mr J. H. Kramer Chief, Operations Review Unit	Ministry of Foreign Affairs Directorate-General International Co-operation Casuariestraat 16 The Hague, Netherlands
13	Mr J. Loup Sous-Directeur des Etudes du Développement	Ministère des Relations Extérieures Services Coopération et Développement 20 Rue Monsieur 75700 Paris, France
14	Prof E. Luzzadi Consultant	Ministry of Foreign Affairs Rome, Italy (University of Turin)
15	Mr P. G. Rwelamira Economist, Evaluation Department	African Development Bank (AfDB) BP 1387, Abidjan 01 Ivory Coast
16	Mr A. Sanguini Consigliere	Dipartimento Cooperazione Sviluppo Via Piere di Cadoze, 30 Rome, Italy
17	Mr Z. M. Santiago Chief Evaluation Officer Special Programmes Branch	Canadian International Development Agency (CIDA) 200 Promenade du Portage Hull, Quebec Canada, K1A 0G4
18	Mr G. Schwab Evaluation Officer, Bureau of Programming and Management	International Labour Organisation (ILO) CH-1211 Geneva 22 Switzerland
19	Dr S. M. Shah Adviser (Evaluation), Programme Evaluation Organisation	Planning Commission Government of India New Delhi, India
20	Mr M. Tobin	United Nations Conference on Trade and Development (UNCTAD) Geneva, Switzerland
21	Mr T. Van Banning	Bureau of Bilateral Aid Ministry of Foreign Affairs Directorate-General International Co-operation Casauriestraat 16 The Hague, Netherlands

22	Mr R. Vanore Assistant Secretary General	Society for International Development (SID) Palazzo Della Cavilta del Lavoro 00144 Rome, Italy
23	Mr M. L. Weiner Director-General, Operations Evaluation	World Bank 1818 H Street, NW Washington DC 20433, USA
24	Mr J. White Principal Administrator, DAC Expert Group on Aid Evaluation	Development Cooperation Directorate Organisation for Economic Cooperation and Development (OECD) 2 Rue André Pascal 75775 Paris, Cedex 16 France
25	Mr K. Winkel Head, Evaluation Unit	Danish International Development Agency (DANIDA) Asiatisk Plans 2 1440 Copenhagen, Denmark

High Commissions/Embassies

26	Mr A. Saifuddin Minister (Economic & Commercial)	High Commission for the People's Republic of Bangladesh 28 Queen's Gate London, England SW7 5JA
27	Mr B. Simorangkir	Indonesian Embassy 38 Grosvenor Square London, England W1X 9AD
28	Mr D. Sutjiptohardjo Economic Department	Indonesian Embassy 38 Grosvenor Square London, England W1X 9AD
29	Mr G. A. J. Pida First Secretary	Malawi High Commission 33 Grosvenor Street London, England W1X 0DE

Universities/Institutes

30	Mr D. G. R. Belshaw Dean & Leader Agricultural Economics	School of Development Studies University of East Anglia Norwich, England NR4 7TJ
31	Dr I. Carruthers Reader in Agrarian Development	Wye College University of London Ashford, Kent, England
32	Prof D. Colman Agricultural Economics	Manchester University Manchester, England M13 9PL

33	Mr K. Crean Principal Lecturer	Centre for Fisheries Studies Humberside College of Higher Education Cottingham Road Hull, England HU6 7RT
34	Dr G. B. Edwards Senior Lecturer in Economics	School of Development Studies University of East Anglia Norwich, England NR4 7TJ
35	Prof D. Edwards	Project Planning Centre for Developing Countries University of Bradford Bradford, England BD7 1DP
36	Prof M. Faber Director	Institute of Development Studies (IDS) University of Sussex Brighton, Sussex, England BN1 9RE
37	Mr T. W. Gee Secretary	Institute of Development Studies (IDS) University of Sussex Brighton, Sussex, England BN1 9RE
38	Mrs M. G. W. Hardiman Senior Lecturer in Social Administration	London School of Economics and Political Science (LSE) Houghton Street, Aldwych London, England WC2A 2AE
39	Mr A. Jennings Department of Economics	University of Leicester Leicester, England
40	Dr R. M. Lawson Consultant Fisheries Economist	Centre for Fisheries Studies Humberside College of Higher Education Cottingham Road Hull, England HU6 7RT
41	Prof M. Lipton	Institute of Development Studies University of Sussex
42	Mr D. McNeill	Development Planning Unit University College, London Endsleigh Gardens London, England WC1H 0ED
43	Dr J. Majumdar Senior Lecturer	Project Planning Centre for Developing Countries University of Bradford Bradford, England BD7 1DP
44	Mr S. Maxwell Research Fellow	Institute of Development Studies (IDS) University of Sussex Brighton, Sussex, England BN1 9RE
45	Dr P. Mosley Lecturer in Economics	University of Bath Claverton Down Bath, England BA2 7AY

46	Dr I. Simpson	University of Leeds School of Economics Studies Leeds, England
47	Dr M. Simpson	University of Leeds School of Economics Studies Leeds, England
48	Mr L. P. Taylor Tutor in Development Studies	Selly Oak Colleges Birmingham, England BZ9 6LQ
49	Mr D. S. Thornton Reader	University of Reading Department of Agricultural Economics 4 Earley Gate, Whiteknights Road Reading, England
50	Dr P. Vaughan Snr Lecturer, Health Care and Epidemiology Co-ordinator, Evaluation and Planning Centre	Ross Institute of Tropical Hygiene London School of Hygiene and Tropical Medicine Keppel Street London, England WC1E 7HT
51	Mr D. Wall	International Economics Research Centre University of Sussex Brighton, England BN1 9QN
52	Dr G. Walt Research Fellow in Health Policy (Evaluation)	Ross Institute of Tropical Hygiene London School of Hygiene and Tropical Medicine Keppel Street London, England WC1E 7HT
53	Mr M. Whitby Reader in Rural Resource Development	Department of Agricultural Economics University of Newcastle Newcastle upon Tyne England NE1 7RU
54	Prof P. R. C. Williams	Department of Education in Developing Countries University of London Institute of Education Bedford Way, London England WC1H 0AL
55	Mr P. J. Wood Head, Unit of Tropical Silviculture	Department of Forestry University of Oxford South Parks Road Oxford, England OX1 3RB
56	Dr C. L. Colclough	Institute of Development Studies University of Sussex Brighton, England BN1 9RE

ODA Personnel

57	Mr D. Boughton	Natural Resources
58	Mr C. N. Britton	Executive Officer, Evaluation Department
59	Mr R. A. Browning	Deputy Secretary
60	Mr J. L. F. Buist	Under Secretary, Africa Division
61	Dr S. Conlin	Social Development Adviser
62	Miss G. M. Cortazzi	Information Department
63	Dr B. E. Cracknell	Senior Economic Adviser and Head, Evaluation Department
64	Dr R. K. Cunningham	Chief Adviser, Natural Resources
65	Mr W. A. Dodd	Chief Education Adviser, Education Division
66	Mr M. B. Grieveson	Principal Engineering Adviser, Engineering Division
67	Mr K. D. Grimshaw	Principal, Evaluation Department
68	Dr G. D. Gwyer	Natural Resources Economics and Management Adviser
69	Dr D. N. F. Hall	Principal Fisheries Adviser
70	Dr D. W. Hall	Environment Adviser
71	Mr R. H. Kemp	Forestry Adviser
72	Mr A. A. Kingshotte	Corps of Specialists, Evaluation Department
73	Mr G. P. McCann	Agricultural Economist
74	Mrs T. Platt	Clerical Officer, Evaluation Department
75	Mr R. S. Porter	Deputy Secretary and Chief Economist
76	Mr A. Smith	Senior Economic Adviser, Evaluation Department
77	Dr T. Spens	Senior Social Development Adviser
78	Mr J. N. Stevens	Economic Adviser, Evaluation Department
79	Mr B. P. Thomson	Economic Adviser, Evaluation Department
80	Mr G. Wadhwa	Assistant Information Officer, Information Department
81	Mr J. K. Wright	Under Secretary, Economic Service

ODA-Associated Bodies and Scientific Units

82 Mr R. D. Bell
    Head, Overseas Division

National Institute of Agricultural
Engineering (NIAE)
Wrest Park, Silsoe,
Bedfordshire, England MK45 4HS

83 Mr J. W. F. Dowling
    Principal Scientific
    Officer

Transport and Road Research
Laboratory (TRRL)
Old Wokingham Road
Crowthorne, Berkshire, England

84 Mr J. L. Hine
    Senior Scientific Officer

Transport and Road Research
Laboratory (TRRL)
Old Wokingham Road
Crowthorne, Berkshire, England

85 Mr I. G. Hughes
    Assistant Director
    Head, Overseas Division

Institute of Geological Sciences (IGS)*
Nicker Hill, Keyworth
Nottingham, England NG12 5GG

86 Mr R. Jarvis

British Council
10 Spring Gardens
London, England SW1A 2BN

87 Dr N. Kemp

British Council
10 Spring Gardens
London, England SW1A 2BN

88 Mr K. O'Connor
    Education Officer

British Council
10 Spring Gardens
London, England SW1A 2BN

89 Mr C. A. Robertson
    Assistant Director

Land Resources Development Centre
(LRDC)
Tolworth Tower
Surbiton, Surrey, England

90 Mr D. Brewin
    Adviser on Technical
    Education

TETOC, British Council
10 Spring Gardens
London, England SW1A 2BN

91 Mr A. Thomas
    Assistant Director, TCTD

British Council
10 Spring Gardens
London, England SW1A 2BN

92 Mrs J. M. White
    Economic Adviser

Transport and Road Research
Laboratory (TRRL)
Overseas Unit
Old Wokingham Road
Crowthorne, Berkshire, England

93 Mr R. F. L. Wilkins
    Head Group A

Higher Education Division
British Council
10 Spring Gardens
London, England SW1A 2BN

* Now the British Geological Survey

94 Mrs S. Wilson
    Projects Officer

TETOC
Science, Technology and Education
Division, British Council
10 Spring Gardens
London, England SW1A 2BN

95 Mr T. J. Willcocks

National Institute of Agricultural
Engineering (NIAE)
Silsoe, Bedfordshire
England MK45 4HS

Consultants

96 Dr M. J. Barber
    Managing Director

British Mining Consultants Ltd
P.O. Box 18, Mill Lane
Huthwaite, Sutton-in-Ashfield
Nottinghamshire, England NG17 2NS

97 Mr W. Bor
    Chief Planning Consultant

Llewelyn-Davies Weeks
Brook House
2–16 Torrington Place
London, England WC1E 7HN

98 Mr S. R. Dines
    President

Samuel R. Dines International
108 North Main
Lugan, Utah 84321, USA

99 Mr D. M. Finlayson
    Director

Aspinwall Hydrotechnical Services Ltd
Pengwern Court
High Street, Shrewsbury
Shropshire, England SY1 1SR

100 Mr C. E. Finney
    Chief Economist

Hunting Technical Services Ltd
Elstree Way, Borehamwood
Herts, England WD6 1SB

101 Mr A. J. Jacobs

Watson Hawksley
Terriers House
Amersham Road, High Wycombe
Bucks, England HP13 5AJ

102 Mr J. C. Judson
    Director

W. S. Atkins Group Consultants
Woodcote Grove, Ashley Road
Epsom, Surrey, England KT18 5BS

103 Mr P. J. Kettle
    Senior Consultant

Transmark
45 Seymour Street
London, England W1H 5AE

104 Mr C. T. Lovick
    Partner

Oscar Faber Partnership
Marlborough House
Upper Marlborough Road
St Albans, England AL1 3UT

105 Mr P. E. McGowan Director	Mackay and Schnellmann Ltd Lincoln House 296–302 High Holborn London, England WC1V 7JJ
106 Mr J. D. Mettam Senior Partner	Bertlin and Partners, Civil Engineers Congreve House 86 Station Road Redhill, Surrey, England RH1 1PL
107 Mr T. P. O'Sullivan Partner	T. P. O'Sullivan and Partners 56–58 Putney High Street London, England SW15 1SF
108 Miss M. A. Pettit Senior Intelligence Officer	W. S. Atkins Group, Consultants Woodcote Grove Ashley Road Epsom, Surrey, England KT18 5BS
109 Mr I. C. Price Associate	Sir William Halcrow and Partners Burderop Park Swindon, Wilts, England SN4 0QD
110 Mr P. M. Prynn Director (Economics)	Halcrow Fox and Associates 3 Shortlands, Hammersmith London, England W6 8DJ
111 Mr I. D. Richardson Managing Director	Fisheries Development Ltd 37 Queen Street London, England EC4R 1BY
112 Mr M. Shenfield Director (Economics Studies)	Travers-Morgan International 136 Long Acre London, England WC2E 9AE
113 Mr R. Varley Senior Economist	Hunting Technical Services Elstree Way, Borehamwood Herts, England WD6 1SB
114 Mr R. Weatherell Associate	T. P. O'Sullivan and Partners 56–58 Putney High Street London, England SW15 1SF
115 Mr S. R. Wilson Agricultural Economist	Muir Wilson International 8 Stanley Crescent London, England W11 2NB
116 Mr J. Woodford	Penrose Associates 14–15 Waterloo Street Bristol, England BS8 4BT
117 Mr P. J. Woolland Partner	Lemon and Blizard Telford House, Hulse Road Southampton, England SO9 3JQ
118 Mr J. Jacobs Freelance Consultant	Horseshoe House Beckley, Rye East Sussex, England

Miscellaneous

119 Mr D. R. Drabble
   Planning Executive

Commonwealth Development
Corporation (CDC)
33 Hill Street
London, England W1A 3AR

120 Mr D. Frost
   Chief Executive

Intermediate Technology Department
Group Ltd (ITDG)
9 King Street
London, England WC2E 8HN

121 Mr K. V. Henderson
   formerly Director of
   Statistics, ODA

45 Chester Road
Wimbledon
London, England SW19 4TS

122 Mr T. Killick
   Director

Overseas Development Institute (ODI)
10–11 Percy Street
London, England W1P 0JB

123 Mr J. P. Richards
   Deputy Director

Voluntary Service Overseas (VSO)
9 Belgrave Square
London, England SW1X 8PW

124 Mr D. Richardson
   Director

International Labour Office (ILO)
96–98 Marsham Street
London, England SW1P 4LY

125 Mr L. N. Robertson
   Agricultural Adviser

Crown Agents for Oversea
Governments and Administrations
4 Millbank
London, England SW1P 3JD

126 Dr M. Stiernborg
   Director Evaluation

International Planned Parenthood
Federation (IPPF)
18–20 Lower Regent Street
London, England SW1Y 4PW

127 Mr M. R. Walsh
   Corporate Planner

Crown Agents for Oversea
Governments and Administrations
4 Millbank
London, England SW1P 3JD

128 Mr D. Nelson
   Editor

Gemini News Service
40–53 Fleet Street
London, England EC4Y 1BT

APPENDIX III
Conference Programme

Thursday 7 April 1983

10.00 a.m.   ODA's Evaluation System
(Chairman: Mr R. A. Browning, Deputy Secretary)
Basic Objectives _Mr R. A. Browning_
The System Described _Dr B. E. Cracknell_
Feedback of Results _Mr J. K. Wright_

11.15 a.m.   Coffee/Tea

11.45 a.m.   Open Discussion on above

12.45 a.m.   Lunch

Afternoon

2.15 p.m.   Some Problem Areas in Evaluation
(Chairman: Mr J. K. Wright, Under Secretary, Economic Service)
Topics introduced by members of Evaluation Department
will include:
The Different Objectives of Evaluation
The Relationship between Monitoring and Evaluation
Baseline Studies
The Role of Impact Assessment
The Role of Recipient Countries
Criteria for Selecting Projects for Evaluation
Choice of Evaluators
Confidentiality of Reports

3.15 p.m.   Tea/Coffee

3.45 p.m.   Open Discussion on above

Evening

6.00 p.m.   Sherry Party
Hosted by Prof M. Faber, Director of IDS

7.15 p.m.   Buffet Supper _Hosted by ODA_

Friday 8 April 1983

9.30 a.m.	Key Findings from ODA Evaluations by Sector

9.30 a.m.   Key Findings from ODA Evaluations by Sector
(Chairman: Mr R. S. Porter, Deputy Secretary and Chief Economist)

Capital Projects:
1 Natural Resources and Rural Development   *Dr G. Gwyer*
2 Infrastructure   *Mrs J. White*

10.15 a.m.   Open Discussion on above

11.00 a.m.   Coffee/Tea

11.30 a.m.   3 Technical Co-operation   *Mr A. Thomas, British Council*
                  4 Programme Aid   *Mr B. Thomson, Evaluation Department*

12.15 p.m.   Open Discussion on above

12.45 p.m.   Lunch

Afternoon

2.15 p.m.   Evaluation Systems of other Donors and Developing Countries
(Chairman: Mr R. A. Browning, Deputy Secretary)

IBRD   *Mr M. L. Weiner, Director-General, Operations Evaluations Dept*

USAID   *Ms M. Hageboeck, Division Chief, Programme Evaluation*

Indian Evaluation Service   *Dr S. M. Shah, Adviser (Evaluation), Planning Commission, New Delhi*

3.45 p.m.   Tea/Coffee

4.00 p.m.   Open Discussion on above

5.00 p.m.   Quo Vadis? A Visionary Look at where Evaluation is Heading in the Years Ahead
Mr R. J. Berg, Overseas Development Council, Washington, USA

5.15 p.m.   Closing Address
Mr R. S. Porter, Deputy Secretary and Chief Economist

5.30 p.m.   Conference ends